YOUNG ARCHITECTS 15:
RANGE

Young Architects 15
Range

Foreword by Charles Waldheim
Introduction by Anne Rieselbach

LCLA Office
Matter Design
MARC FORNES / THEVERYMANY
PRAUD
SJET
Young Projects

Princeton Architectural Press
The Architectural League of New York

Published by:
Princeton Architectural Press
37 East Seventh Street
New York, New York 10003
www.papress.com

To view podcast interviews
with each firm, please visit the
Architectural League's website
at www.archleague.org.

Editor: Meredith Baber
Cover design: Pentagram
Interior layout: Elana Schlenker and
Benjamin English

Special thanks to: Mariam Aldhahi,
Sara Bader, Nicola Bednarek Brower,
Janet Behning, Megan Carey,
Carina Cha, Andrea Chlad,
Barbara Darko, Russell Fernandez,
Will Foster, Jan Haux, Diane Levinson,
Jennifer Lippert, Katharine Myers,
Jamie Nelson, Lauren Palmer,
Jay Sacher, Rob Shaeffer,
Andrew Stepanian, Sara Stemen,
Marielle Suba, Paul Wagner,
and Joseph Weston of Princeton
Architectural Press
—Kevin C. Lippert, publisher

This publication is supported,
in part, by public funds from the
New York City Department of Cultural
Affairs in partnership with the City
Council and the New York State
Council on the Arts with the support
of Governor Andrew Cuomo and
the New York State Legislature.

Installation photos at
Parsons The New School for Design
© David Sundberg / ESTO

Library of Congress
Cataloging-in-Publication Data:
Young architects 15: range / foreword
by Charles Waldheim; introduction by
Anne Rieselbach. — First edition.
    pages cm. — (Young architects; 15)
ISBN 978-1-61689-239-5 (pbk.)
1. Architectural League Prize for Young
Architects and Designers—Exhibi-
tions. 2. Architecture—Awards—
United States. 3. Architecture—United
States—History—21st century.
4. Young architects—United States.
I. Waldheim, Charles, writer of
supplementary textual content.
II. Rieselbach, Anne, writer of
introduction. III. Callejas, Luis,
1981– author. LCLA Office.
IV. Architectural League of New York.
V. Title: Range.
NA2340.Y679955 2014
720.79'73—dc23
                                   2013043212

CONTENTS

8 Acknowledgments

9 Foreword **Charles Waldheim**

12 Introduction **Anne Rieselbach**

17 Biographies

20 **LCLA Office**
Luis Callejas

46 **Matter Design**
Brandon Clifford and Wes McGee

72 **MARC FORNES / THEVERYMANY**
Marc Fornes

98 **PRAUD**
Rafael Luna and Dongwoo Yim

124 **SJET**
Skylar J. E. Tibbits

150 **Young Projects**
Bryan Young

ACKNOWLEDGMENTS

Annabelle Selldorf, President, The Architectural League of New York

Each program year at the Architectural League ends, in a sense, at the beginning, spotlighting the work of the winners of the Architectural League Prize for Young Architects + Designers. The winners, just starting to spring away from their academic roots and mentors' influence, are clearly launched on a strong trajectory!

This year's program, Range, was the thirty-second annual lecture series and exhibition of work by the League Prize competition winners. Young designers, ten years or less out of undergraduate or graduate school who are residents of North America, are invited to submit a portfolio, accompanied by a text that addresses the competition theme composed by the League Prize Committee—a group of past winners who organize the competition with the League staff. In addition to creating a site-specific installation of their work and presenting a lecture, winners engage in interviews that, along with an edited video of their lecture, are published on the League's website, and compile images of their work to expand their ideas for this annual catalog.

The theme changes each year to address current issues in architectural design and theory. The committee also asks prominent members of the design community to serve with them as competition jurors. I would like to thank committee members Benjamin Aranda, Seung Teak Lee, and Michael Szivos, and jurors Teresita Fernandez, Paul Lewis, Thom Mayne, Charles Waldheim, and Meejin Yoon for their time and insight, which shaped such a compelling group of winning work.

Thanks also to Michael Bierut and Britt Cobb of Pentagram, who once again designed competition and exhibition graphics to express the theme, David Sundberg of ESTO whose photographs uniquely captured the exhibition, the editors at Princeton Architectural Press for their skillful preparation of this publication, and Parsons the New School for Design exhibition and events staff—Radhika Subramanian, Kristina Kaufman, and Daisy Wong—who generously provided their expertise to guide the installation and lectures.

Dedicated supporters make this program possible. We thank Dornbracht, Tishler und Sohn, Susan Grant Lewin Associates, Microsol Resources, and Monadnock Construction, Inc., for their generosity. The League Prize is also supported by the Next Generation Fund of the Architectural League. League programs are additionally supported in part by public funds from the New York City Department of Cultural Affairs in partnership with the City Council and the New York State Council on the Arts with the support of Governor Andrew Cuomo and the New York State Legislature.

FOREWORD: NATURAL SELECTIONS

Charles Waldheim

The 2013 Architectural League Prize was awarded to six diverse practices composed of eight talented young architects. The work of these architects was selected from an astonishing pile of portfolios gathered in response to a call for "Range" in contemporary practice. At first glance, the body of submissions presented a false choice between two seemingly divergent cultural propositions. On the one hand, the jury was confronted with a majority of projects interested in a self-conscious similarity of the kind that is hard to avoid these days. On the other hand, the jury encountered a minority position of practices engaged in a seemingly self-satisfied social or environmental instrumentality. In response, the jury initially murmured about a paucity of programmatic invention or typological analysis. These initial misgivings gave way to fully formed fulminations on the rarity of political position evident in the work. Then lunch arrived, and things began to get more interesting.

After several hours of isolated scrutiny, followed by several more hours engaged in collective consensus building, patterns began to emerge. Almost exclusively those patterns could be seen as having emerged from the study of the natural world. In spite of their apparent stylistic and thematic diversity, the various practices awarded the 2013 League Prize are unanimous in their (conscious or subconscious) use of models and metaphors from the natural world. Admittedly, the emulation of natural models can be found across the depth and breadth of material submitted for consideration by the League Prize jury. However, it is especially evident in the work of this year's League Prize winners. This invocation of natural order can be found in Matter Design's interest in states of matter and material properties as well as the formal structure of Bryan Young's various references to nonhuman construction. An interest in modeling the natural certainly informs SJET's line of self-assembling, semiautonomous architectonic particles, as well the morphology and genesis of PRAUD's typological inventions. The modeling of the natural world can equally be found in MARC FORNES / THEVERYMANY's sculptural surfaces and foamy furnishings and Luis Callejas's hydrological fantasies and aeronautical obsessions. Collectively the work of the 2013 League Prize winners (unsurprisingly) invokes the ecological model. What may be more interesting is that this modeling of the natural world is most often absent from any explicit environmentalism. This has much to do with the curious confluence of criticality and ecological thinking in architectural culture.

Of the various models built from the natural world, ecology has emerged as among the most important epistemological frameworks of our age. This claim is based on the fact that ecology has transcended its origins as a natural science to encompass a diverse range of meanings across the natural and social sciences, history and the humanities, design and the arts. From its origins as a protodisciplinary branch of biology in the nineteenth century, ecology developed into a modern science in the twentieth century and increasingly toward a multidisciplinary intellectual framework in the first two decades of the twenty-first century. This disciplinary promiscuity is not without its intellectual or practical problems. The slippage of ecology from natural science to cultural lens remains a source of confusion across the design disciplines, not least within architecture.

Much contemporary design practice begins with the enduring understanding of ecology as offering a model of the natural world. This most fundamental definition is evident in the work of Richard Forman and Eugene Odum, among others. It continues to apply, as ecology is understood as offering models to predict and account for the natural world. Over the past several decades, ecology has been found relevant as an epistemological framework operating at the level of a metaphor in the social or human sciences, the humanities, history, philosophy, and the arts. References to ecology in the work of Gregory Bateson, Giorgio Agamben, and Felix Guattari, to name but a few, illustrate the fecundity of ecological thinking across a range of fields. This metaphorical understanding of ecology has been particularly significant for design discourse, as it has informed architectural theory and design culture.

At least since Peter Eisenman's post-functionalism argument of the mid-1970s, architecture has relied upon the putatively critical denial of utility as a basis for its cultural value. This suppression of commodity and use value has also expressed itself as a claim for the "autonomy" of architectural culture, articulated as a form of resistance to architecture's engagements with the social, political, and economic. Over the past decade, as architecture's implication in questions of environment and climate have returned to the fore, many have argued for the maintenance of the critical cultural project of autonomy, as opposed to instrumentality. This has often been articulated as a project of ongoing resistance to architecture's entanglement in the "externalities" of energy and environment, among others. From this point of view, questions of climate are often viewed as a pure externality to architecture's cultural value, as defined through its self-imposed alienation from instrumental impact.

Over the past decade the project of criticality has been confronted on another flank, with the proposition of a so-called "post-critical" position that espouses mood, cultural commodity, and "design intelligence" over distanced authorship. The work recognized by the 2013 League Prize offers the potential of a third term in these debates, avoiding pure opposition in favor of an opening toward a projective, if not precisely redemptive, project for contemporary architecture. This work suggests the potential for an architecture of often radically distanced authorship arrived at through highly measured performative parameters. This "alienation" or decentering of authorship, while not without its antecedents in contemporary architectural culture, is radically distinct in that it occludes simple visibility of effect, in favor of a more complex array of ecological orders. Often, these orders are the result of highly choreographed yet persistently nonlinear and indeterminate relational transactions between species and their environments over time. This is particularly evident in the generation of architectural production embodied in this year's League Prize submissions. As the original call for entries to the 2013 League Prize claimed, "architecture seems without bounds right now." Yes it does, almost as boundless as the natural world that serves as its model today.

INTRODUCTION

Anne Rieselbach, Program Director, The Architectural League of New York

Your range has the ability not only to define your work but also the practice of architecture as a whole.

How can new design approaches redefine architectural practice? What are the potential implications for design? This year's theme, "Range," reflected the League Prize committee's observation that young architects' skills have diversified at a rapid pace that "sometimes exceeds the expansion of project types, pragmatic as well as speculative." They identified how this expertise can inspire explorations of "potential boundaries with practices that are radical…that search the edges of the discipline to find its limits." The committee encouraged entrants to express "the range they operate within and how that range reacts as they encounter perceived limits of the profession."

The competition winners compellingly answered the committee's call to elucidate the invention driving their work. Each of their portfolios contained a range of projects that pushed traditional boundaries of practice, in keeping with categories outlined in the call for entries, from "formal treatments, construction, paradigm shifts, material experiments, and applications at a variety of scales" to the location of their work. The winners chose two distinct ways to exemplify their design approaches for the League Prize exhibition, either presenting a collection of projects that provided the armature to trace the development of their design approach or producing a single project expanding on earlier work.

Drawing sets, photographs, and different model types for Bryan Young's projects—such as the Hive Lantern, a freestanding fireplace set in the Canadian landscape, a New York City townhouse and loft, and a retreat in the Dominican Republic, all built or under construction this year—illustrated his firm Young Projects' synthesis of digital and traditional building techniques. A large two-part model of the Playa Grande Main House demonstrated the formal relationship of the complex roof geometry to the house and site. The lower portion addressed the site topography, massing of the house, and the flowing geometry of the scissor trusses. Suspended above the model, the roof demonstrated "the graphic pattern which emerges from the collision of simple rules of fabrication and the surface geometry of the roof."

Sinuous CNC-milled birch plywood shelves with integral brackets, part of a modular system produced by Brandon Clifford and Wes McGee of Matter Design, supported models of their firm's prototypes and realized architectural projects—which range in size from a sixty-foot foam tower to a twenty-four-foot concrete spiral stair to a full-scale experimental volumetric vault to their Cumulous jewelry series—as well as copies of a catalog created for the exhibition. The publication compiles the past five years of the firm's projects in reverse chronological order, articulating their efforts to privilege volume over surface in the generation of form.

The movement of 350 hollow spheres submerged in a 200-gallon water-filled tank provided the means for SJET's Skylar J.E. Tibbits to test his ongoing investigation of nondeterministic self-assembly. Within the transparent spheres, internal armatures containing tetrahedral magnets and lead shot created covalent bonding geometries between atoms. Intermolecular forces drove the spheres to interact with one another, forming two-dimensional and three-dimensional structures. The dynamic self-assembly of the system enacted a material phase change between crystalline solids, liquids, and gases. Pump-driven water turbulence introduced energy into the system, increasing the entropy and allowing structures to self-assemble. Formal order and reconfiguration oscillated based on the competition between the strength of the intermolecular bonds and the energy of the system.

Rafael Luna and Dongwoo Yim chose to graphically articulate their firm PRAUD's multifaceted practice by mapping its internal structure as a way to represent their broad range of work. A large vinyl graphic, punctuated by images of theoretical projects, realized work, and text as well as by shelves holding the firm's publications, was organized by building types stretched along a carefully calibrated timeline. Read chronologically from left to right, the linear diagram systematically tracked their categories of work: research, architecture, urbanism, and design. If read from right to left, irregular curvilinear paths reconfigure the strict linear orientation, demonstrating how a project can be recategorized based on the range of the architects' roles as practitioner, dreamer, and theorist.

Five suspended large-scale figures, "(re)investigated the art of tailoring and sewing patterns through computation, digital fabrication, and craft…," creating forms that Marc Fornes of MARC FORNES / THEVERYMANY describes as "somewhere between garments and body armor." The project investigated different ways to precisely tailor custom aluminum garments through a computational set of instructions, or "protocols," which are applied onto digital bodies in motion. Building on the precedent of the firm's previous work, different search algorithms were developed resulting in a collection of unique parts CNC-milled from aluminum

sheets and precisely hand-riveted to create a human scale "second skin," essentially completing a set of three-dimensional puzzles. The resulting anthropomorphic forms swayed and seemingly interacted, charging and defining space.

A slim "waterline" stretched across the gallery wall oriented images of Luis Callejas's master plan for islands along Kiev's Dnieper River, locating the elevation of each aquatic or airborne project. Similarly oriented along the waterline, intricately detailed topographic contour models offered details of "microtactical" interventions for the islands' structures and pathways. Additional images illustrated other projects by his firm LCLA Office, including a master plan for the Olympic Park in Rio de Janeiro, the Airplot project in London, a proposal for reclaiming the Serrana and Quita Sueño islands in the San Andrés archipelago, and his first realized work, the aquatic center in Medellín, Colombia, designed in collaboration with Edgar Mazo and Sebastián Mejia, as well as the studio's most recent publication, *Pamphlet Architecture 33: Islands and Atolls*, paired with plans of the firm's work drawn by Melissa Naranjo.

The competition winners' work on display demonstrated their abilities to range within and beyond traditional boundaries of architectural site, form, and practice. Their projects varied in design approach and in scale from objects to structures to local and regional designs, on the surface, aloft, and underwater. Whether reconfiguring architectural elements and structure, reshaping typological form, testing new materials and fabrication methods, or inventing new ways to generate form, the surprising range of design approaches and realized work exemplified the League Prize Committee's open-ended description of the profession, "architecture seems without bounds right now. It can be anything."

BIOGRAPHIES

LCLA Office was founded by Luis Callejas and is based in Cambridge, Massachusetts, with an office run by Melissa Naranjo in Medellín, Colombia. The practice, positioned at the intersections of the fields of landscape, architecture, and urbanism, explores "new forms of public realms through environmental and territorial operations," such as the *Tactical Archipelago* project in Kiev, Ukraine. There, LCLA reconsidered thirty-seven islands in the city's Dnieper River as places for recreation, ecological infrastructure, transportation, and, through a series of microclusters inserted on the river's surface, itinerant zones of activity and services. Other recent projects include his collaboration with Edgar Mazo and Sebastián Mejia, as the firm Paisajes Emergentes, to complete the Aquatic Center for the 2010 South American Games and the renovation of the main soccer stadium in Bogotá, Colombia. Callejas received a degree in architecture from the Universidad Nacional de Colombia in 2008 and currently teaches Landscape Architecture at the Harvard Graduate School of Design.

Matter Design combines Brandon Clifford's "dedication to design" and Wes McGee's "proficiency in fabrication," placing the studio at the confluence of several contrasts: drawing versus making, digital versus physical. Described by its principals as an "interdisciplinary academic research studio dedicated to reimagining the role of the architect in the digital era," Matter Design explores such issues as volume over surface and the usage of scale experiments to adapt the tenets of masonry construction to contemporary methods of construction. Clifford received a BS in Architecture from the Georgia Institute of Technology and an MArch from Princeton University and teaches at Massachusetts Institute of Technology. McGee received a BS in Mechanical Engineering and an MID from the Georgia Institute of Technology and is currently an assistant professor and the director of the FABLab at the University of Michigan Taubman College of Architecture and Urban Planning.

MARC FORNES / THEVERYMANY, based in Brooklyn, is a leader in the development of computation applied to design and digital fabrication. He realizes geometrically complex and self-supporting structures for both artistic and commercial settings, from pop-up stores to gallery installations to park pavilions. Though composed of flat elements, Fornes's digitally designed skins appear to undulate, simultaneously acting as both surface and support. With an emphasis on prototypical architecture as a test proof of digital design, MARC FORNES / THEVERYMANY develops custom protocols, or sets of deterministic algorithmic steps, encoded within a computational syntax. The resulting morphologies are strictly controlled yet curiously undetermined until the code is ultmiately executed. His prototypes have been displayed as part of the permanent collections of the Centre Pompidou and the Centre National des Arts Plastiques (CNAP), both in Paris, and the FRAC Centre in Orleans, France. Fornes received an MArch in architecture and urbanism from the Design Research Lab of the Architectural Association in London and has taught at Columbia University, Princeton University, Harvard University, and the University of Michigan.

PRAUD, founded by Rafael Luna and Dongwoo Yim and based in Boston and Seoul, focuses on the interplay between topology and typology as a means of understanding urban development and morphology in their work. The office experiments with reconfiguration, the relationship between solid and void, and the opportunities created by overlapping structural and spatial functions. Their holistic view of the architect as a researcher, practitioner, theorist, and visionary is illustrated by their interest in research and publications, which serve as the generator of what the office calls a "new autonomous language"—an internal logic that produces new expressions of form and function—for contemporary architecture. Luna received a BFA from the Massachusetts College of Art and an MArch from Massachusetts Institute of Technology. Yim received a bachelors degree from Seoul National University and an MArch in Urban Design from the Harvard Graduate School of Design. Luna and Yim have taught at the Rhode Island School of Design.

SJET, a research-based practice in Boston, was founded by Skylar J. E. Tibbits to cross disciplines ranging from architecture and design to fabrication, computer science, and robotics. Tibbits's research interests include self-assembly technologies, programmable materials, and the reinvention of fabrication methods. He has exhibited work at the Guggenheim Museum in New York and the Beijing Biennale and has built large-scale installations in Paris, Calgary, Philadelphia, New York City, Berlin, Frankfurt, and Cambridge. Tibbits received two masters degrees, in Design and Computation and in Computer Science, from the Massachusetts Institute of Technology and a BArch from Philadelphia University. He is a faculty member of MIT's Department of Architecture, teaching masters and undergraduate design studios and coteaching How to Make (Almost) Anything at MIT's Media Lab. Tibbits was awarded the Next Idea Award at Ars Electronica 2013, the Visionary Innovation Award at the Manufacturing Leadership Summit, and a 2012 TED Senior Fellowship, and was named a Revolutionary Mind in *SEED* Magazine's 2008 Design Issue.

Young Projects, the Brooklyn-based design studio, was founded by Bryan Young in 2010. Young Projects investigates the intersection of contemporary digital methods and traditional construction techniques to develop new processes of making and their potential for unique aesthetic expression. The office values the physical constraints of real projects and practices a methodological continuity through the study of material properties and assembly techniques. Young received his BA in Architecture from the University of California, Berkeley, and his MArch with distinction from the Harvard Graduate School of Design, where he was awarded the AIA Henry Adams Medal and the James Templeton Kelley Thesis Prize for his research on diagramming Donkey Kong and Pac-Man. He has taught at Syracuse University and Columbia University, and is currently an adjunct assistant professor of architecture at Parsons the New School for Design.

LCLA OFFICE
Luis Callejas

22	**The River that is not**
26	**Aquatic Center**
28	**Klaksvík City Center Master Plan**
30	**Weatherfields**
32	**Museum of Polish History**
34	**Welcome to Fleetwood**
36	**Airplot**
40	**Tactical Archipelago**

LCLA stands at the intersection of the fields of architecture, landscape, and urbanism, committed to new forms of engagement with the public realm through territorial operations.

By decentralizing the notion of the site, whether airborne or literally at sea, we seek to contrast work that denies context. At the same time our work aligns with the idea that architecture and even landscapes can be autonomous. Thus our projects often radically delimit their qualities, aiming to reveal latent, local conditions isolated from larger territorial and altitudinal conditions.

We declare our commitments to the productive potentials of landscape as a generator of architectural objects. At the same time we believe that landscapes and architectural objects can be the driving force behind large-scale urban interventions. For doing so, architecture needs to work in synchronicity with landscape architecture operations, so that both fields can critically repurpose their traditionally limited disciplinary tools to make a meaningful impact at a territorial scale.

The River that is not

Medellín, Colombia, 2013

Medellín's river is not a river anymore and this condition is reversible. Over the past seventy years the intense processes of urbanization of Medellín and the construction of the canal have transformed the river into nothing more than a canal and the axis for Pan American–transportation infrastructure. Most ideas for renaturalizing the river are naive and impossible.

On the other hand Medellín River is fed by fifty-six small streams that come from the mountains. These streams vary in environmental conditions but some are relatively clean. Our project aims to use the initiative for the restoration of Medellín River as an excuse to deviate public resources from the river to the transformation of Medellín's water streams into public hydric-landscape events. In sync with this initiative, a series of public platforms would be installed on the river without modifying the existing canal. These platforms will host programs that are traditionally contained in public buildings, such as libraries and sports facilities, and will be located at the point where each stream meets with the polluted river.

1: View of platforms on Medellín River

2: Buildings in proximity to creeks are capable of storing water for recreational use

3: Skating platform and public pool on the canal

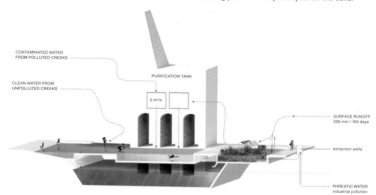

CONTAMINATED WATER
FROM POLLUTED CREEKS

PURIFICATION TANK

CLEAN WATER FROM
UNPOLLUTED CREEKS

2 m³/s

SURFACE RUNOFF
300 mm / 165 days

extraction wells

PHREATIC WATER
industrial pollution

2

3

4: Ideal location of platforms on the twenty-six kilometer canal in relation to water streams
5: Diagram of autonomous platforms with diverse public programs

6: Every building is a water tank capable of treating different volumes of water depending on its location.

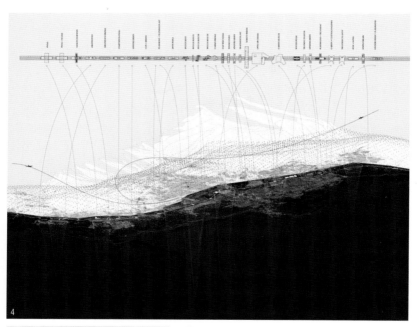

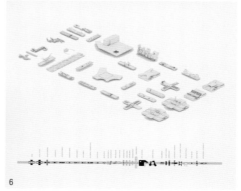

7: Plan of central area and business district
8: Plan of San Fernando water treatment plant used for
public occupation
9: Plan of North plant with remediation areas in proximity
to toxic waste accumulation areas downstream

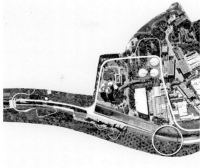

Aquatic Center

Medellín, Colombia, 2010

The new aquatic center was designed to meet the needs of future competitions, and to provide a new swimming teaching facility and public pools.

The project is articulated by gardens through which the four pools are connected. A flooded landscape planted with species typical of tropical wetlands separates private and public spaces.

The program required a complex system of bathrooms and changing rooms for swimmers and the public, which are located beneath the aquatic gardens. A set of courtyards below grade give natural illumination to the private spaces, creating a meeting space and warm-up area for competitors and swimmers.

1: Colombian synchronized swimming team training during 2010 South American Games

2: View of the training pools from the stands
3: Composite image of the aquatic gardens between the pools
4: Composite image of two distinct types of water to separate public and private uses of the complex

Klaksvík City Center Master Plan
Klaksvík, Faroe Islands, 2012

Over the last two hundred years, Klaksvík has grown from five settlements of a mere one hundred people to a modern town of five thousand inhabitants. The large and swift population growth was triggered by the growing fishing industry, which led to the development of areas along the shore for industrial purposes. The central part of town is virtually undeveloped and contains a recent landfill in the area.

Klaksvík's geography is truly remarkable; it is held between two mountains and two bays, and is surrounded by a dramatic landscape. The configuration of the city is equally striking—urban development has historically occurred along the length of the bay, while civic and public institutions have concentrated in the Eiðið—a corridor that runs from one bay to the other, yet fails to directly connect buildings or people with the water. Furthermore, there is little definition to the public spaces surrounding the civic buildings in this area and many of the open spaces lack clear identity or use.

CITY ROOMS
An event landscape proposes to relink the city to both its bays through a sequence of outdoor rooms/landscapes, with development phased over many years. Each of these urban rooms is designed to have a distinct programmatic and landscape character.

The first room is the competition site, which proposes a cultural and civic hub for the city, organized around a new cultural marina that frames the bay and embraces the water. The second room is a hardscaped market space for commercial and residential units and future hotels. The third room, near a school, is conceived as an urban forest planted with junipers and beech to protect against the wind. Farther south, the fourth room consists of expanded playing fields. The fifth room is composed of an education campus anchored by the Klaksvík Technical College, culminating in a promontory to the south bay.

Klaksvík has a rich architectural vernacular—a consistent fabric of individual houses, peaked roofs, and bright colors. The roofscape is punctured with apertures that reflect the colors of the city. Our proposal is inspired by this expressive typology, manipulating form and aggregating cultural buildings to develop a city center that has the capacity to be iconic while integrating into the city fabric.

1: View of Klaksvík city center
2: Plan of the new harbor
3–5: View of the valley with library to the left and
city hall to the right

6: Rendering of different events
7: Aerial view of city center

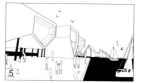

Weatherfields
Abu Dhabi, United Arab Emirates, 2009

Situated along a sandy beachfront in Abu Dhabi between the islands of Yas and
Saadiyat, the project provides a public space capable of harvesting the abundant
renewable resource of wind energy in the Middle East. Unlike current renewable
energy fields where technologies are publicly inaccessible, static, and always
on, this shape-shifting energy generation park offers a range of public engagement
dependent on wind, sun, and moisture. Thus, energy generation becomes a public
performance.

Organized and designed to respond efficiently and creatively to climate, the
park serves as a barometer of regional weather events; it is active during bad weather
and calm when weather is calm, offering a compatible experience in each instance.
It is simultaneously a public space, a dynamic energy icon, and a public weather
service as a registration of daily weather events, such as Shamal winds, dense fog,
and sandstorms.

Unlike large-scale energy infrastructures that are out-of-scale, off-site, and
off-limits, the project and its energy capacity can be employed at the scale of a
single-family home. The two hundred parakites would extend across the test site in
a sixty-meter grid.

With an immense abundance of wind, there is considerable potential for
the Persian Gulf to be the largest renewable energy field in the world and a model
for future regional planning. Weatherfield would become a catalyst for a regional
energy plan in the Middle East and an initial development phase to generate a
large-scale reconsideration of energy in the entire region. This plan proposes the
decommissioning of twentieth-century industrial energy fields across the Persian Gulf
and their transformation into a network of twenty-first-century public energy parks.

1: View of the installation from Dubai

2: Installation during a Shamal storm
3: Different configurations according to weather events
4: Aerial view of the energy generation park from the kites

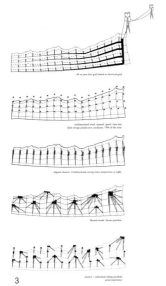

Museum of Polish History
Warsaw, Poland, 2010

The competition for the Museum of Polish History in Warsaw called for a building composed of galleries in which each individual space would be capable of transmitting ideas related to specific historical moments.

These five historical galleries are articulated by a spiral ramp that serves not only as main circulation but also acts as independent exhibition space and a connection between the park and the river shore. The open-air courtyard acts as an extension to the temporal galleries, allowing for large-format exhibitions.

THE GALLERIES
Gallery 1: Medieval era with divided rooms, intricate circulation, and variable
        height and light conditions
Gallery 2: Post-Medieval as one large, open space
Gallery 3: State and culture space divided by exposition walls, open to
        each subgallery
Gallery 4: WWI and WWII galleries for individual or aggregated expositions
Gallery 5: Communist period space contracts and dilates with the repetition
        of a single module

1: View from the park
2: View of the courtyard

3: Medieval gallery
4: Republic-era gallery
5: World War II gallery
6: Communist-era gallery
7: Plan of the park and terraces

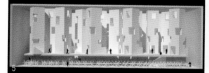

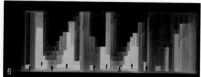

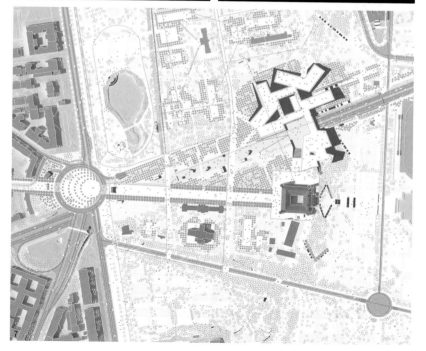

Welcome to Fleetwood
Surrey, Canada, 2009

While the original competition brief called for a welcome sign for the city of Surrey, this project uses a floating tower to expand the agency of a sign into a massive registration of events occurring on the Trans-Canada Highway.

The lighter-than-air tower requires structural support not for its weight but for maintaining its location. Rather than merely display a welcome sign, the Fleetwood Marker employs the benefits of tall vertical structures, such as radio transmission and observation capabilities, opening up potential opportunities in a flat city composed mostly of low-rise buildings and bisected by a highway. Made with clusters of small weather balloons filled with helium, the tower would be the only structure in the city tall enough to facilitate communication antennas. The Fleetwood Marker also acts as a high-altitude public viewing platform, with a gondola at its base for occupation. Finally, a vertical color light show registering highway traffic is rendered on the balloon clusters and corresponds with highway activity, illuminating the installation at night.

1: Trans-Canada Highway with Fleetwood Marker in
the background
2: Plan of central Fleetwood

3: 150-meter high weather balloon tower
4: Image from the gondola over Fleetwood
5: View of the tower from below

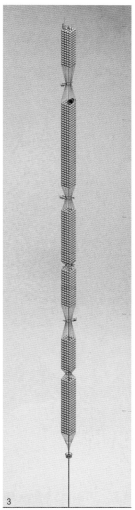

3

4

5

Airplot (or a project for an effective demonstration to stop all air traffic)
London, England, 2009

As part of a strategy to stop air traffic above London's Heathrow Airport, Airplot is a form of airborne intervention and demonstration. The objective of such a barricade is to provide owners of small properties and farms surrounding Heathrow with a tool to halt airport operations to prohibit the construction of Heathrow's third runway.

A "navigation easement" allows property owners or potential purchasers to waive any putative notion of air rights near an airport, for convenience in future real estate transactions as well as to avoid lawsuits from future owners who might claim distress from overflying aircraft. Yet the law recognizes that landowners have property rights in the lower reaches of the airspace above their property. In balancing the public interest in using the airspace for navigation against the landowner's rights, the law declares that landowners own only as much of the airspace above their property as they may reasonably use in connection with their enjoyment of the underlying land. In other words, landowners cannot arbitrarily try to prevent aircraft from flying over their land by erecting spike poles, for example. However, landowners can make legitimate use of their property, even if it interferes with aircraft above the land. Property owners surrounding Heathrow will make a legitimate reclamation of their airspace by launching tethered inflatable copies of objects or even animals.

1: Airborne copies of houses and animals
2: Aerial view of the installation

3: Plan of Heathrow airport and the installation

3

4: View of the installation from the ground

5: Copy of a house using thirty cubic meters of helium
6: Copy of a cow using two cubic meters of helium

Tactical Archipelago
Kiev, Ukraine, 2012

The master plan is articulated through small and tactical operations, or clusters, that can be inserted over time and at specific zones. The deployment of these parts is intended to recover forgotten and unfulfilled citizens' desires—such as taking a bath in the river, walking in the forest, and enjoying clean water—and directly experience Ukrainian nature in the middle of the urban center of Kiev's river coast.

The best way to create a new relationship with such long geography is through the creation of specialized action clusters that will allow the formation of a third zone made out of the transference of water to the firm ground and vice-versa. These clusters support new activities, new landscape references, preservation of weak ecological areas, clean passive energy generation systems, and above all bring the citizens back to the river through new means of participation and leisure.

CLUSTERS
North–south interventions are made to preserve islands to configure a selective landscape production.

SOFT URBANISM, CLUSTERS
The microunits are displayed to show the possibilities of identifying new potentials and to point out imaginative relationships among citizens and the landscape: itinerant inflatable art for energy production, garden barges, and floating infrastructures that can transform zones when needed.

1: Botanical garden island
2: Installation on the bridge

3: Aerial view of the botanical garden island

4: Iceberg park
5: Floating soccer field
6: Botanical garden island barge

7: Aerial view of Hydropak station and interventions in Veliky island

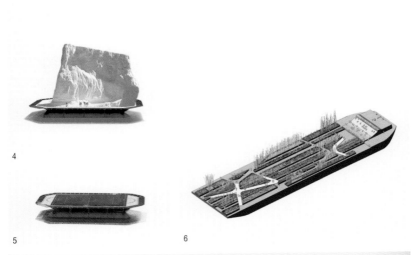

4

5

6

7

8: Underwater view of artificial botanical garden islands
9: Plan of interventions in the city center

10: Different interventions in the Kiev islands located
in the Dnieper River

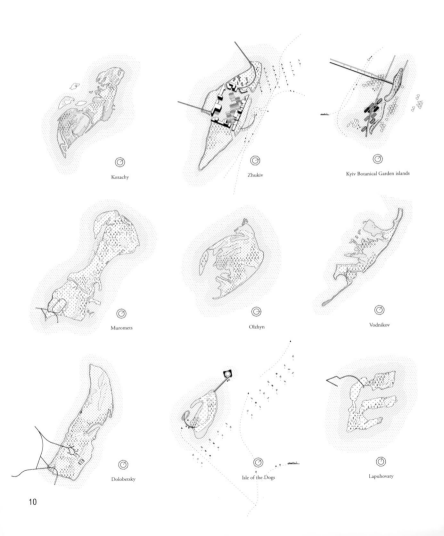

Kozachy

Zhukiv

Kyiv Botanical Garden islands

Muromets

Olzhyn

Vodnikov

Dolobetsky

Isle of the Dogs

Lapuhovaty

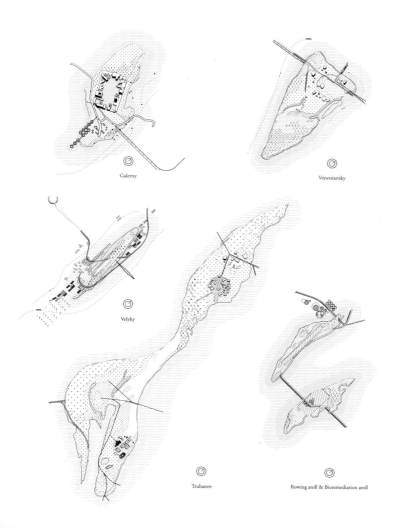

Galerny

Venetsiansky

Velyky

Truhanov

Rowing atoll & Bioremediation atoll

MATTER DESIGN

Brandon Clifford and Wes McGee

48 **Range Exhibition**

50 **Helix**

54 **Cumulus**

56 **La Voûte de LeFevre**

62 **Pongo**

66 **Periscope**

70 **Drawn Dress**

We, a contemporary practice, feel most comfortable situated adjacent to Philibert de l'Orme.[1] Our range is therefore polarized—spanning from ancient to present. We are dedicated to translating ancient (and often lost) methods into contemporary culture. This dedication is best exemplified in our preoccupation with volume. So much of the discussion surrounding digital design has focused on surface, but we leverage past knowledge to better inform this vacuum around volume.

Echoing de l'Orme's trajectory, we produce a series of scale experiments (de l'Orme often used the *trompe* as a vehicle for technical exploration before being appointed as the monarch's architect). These experiments range from a sixty-foot tall foam tower to a compression-only vault to a half-scale helical staircase. Each tackles a chapter in our history of volumetric (stone) architecture—stereotomy, transitions, rhetoric, spirals, tooling, and method. Periscope: Foam Tower mined the past knowledge of stereotomy in order to create developed line carving with a robotic hot-wire. La Voûte de LeFevre is produced with our variable-volumetric calculation to ensure stability. Helix utilizes locking keys, while also addressing issues of weight and balance.

While these projects take part in a trajectory toward a contemporary stone architecture, we retain our obedience to the human body with products such as Pongo and Cumulus. We ourselves build every project we design (another nod to de l'Orme), reimagining the role of the architect to eliminate the segregation of designer from maker by expanding the range of our design practice—builder, theorist, historian, computer, fabricator, author, and thinker.[2]

1: Sixteenth-century architect Philibert de l'Orme was, like Palladio, the son of a mason. He emerged into architecture not through a rigorous understanding of form or technique but as the builder or mason. In his printed work of 1567 *Le premier tome de l'architecture*, de l'Orme introduced the method and definition of *art du trait géométrique*. This method developed as a way to reciprocally draw what can be built and vice versa. Because of this emergence, de l'Orme can also be credited as the first professional architect, as his technique served to instruct and communicate between the designer and the builder, though an important distinction should be drawn between the representation of architecture we now generate and de l'Orme's descriptive geometry that served as a method template for construction. For this reason, we consider de l'Orme to be the predecessor to digital fabrication.

2: Each of these self-assigned disciplines should likely include the prefix of "pseudo," a conceit we are happy to make in preference to the title of dilettante.

Range Exhibition

Architectural League Prize for Young Architects Exhibition
New York, New York, 2013

Matter Design is an interdisciplinary design practice entrenched in the confluence
of digital and material. Our shared interest in design, coupled with proficiency in
the means and methods of production, have led us to collaborate on a range of
experimental projects, which break with conventional disciplinary notions of scale.

Sinuous CNC-milled birch plywood shelves with integral brackets,
part of a modular system titled PlyShelf, support models of architectural projects,
computation prototypes, products, and jewelry. This armature inverts scale by
utilizing full-scale products (plywood) to display models of large projects as small
objects. This inversion produces an understanding of the body of work irrespective
of size or conventional understanding of architectural scale. In addition to
these objects as artifacts, the framework holds copies of a catalog created for
the exhibition. The catalog, titled *Range*, compiles the past five years of the firm's
projects in reverse chronological order, articulating efforts to privilege volume over
surface in the generation of form. This concern was foregrounded in the catalog,
which was designed to elucidate a design process dedicated to the reciprocal
relationship between drawing and making as well as to illustrate the range and
complexity of the work.

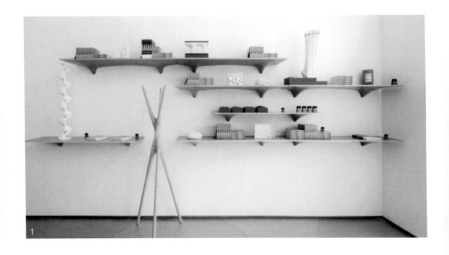

1–2: View of installation

2

Helix

BSA Space, Design Biennial Boston
Boston, Massachusetts, 2013

Our outlook and work demonstrate a preoccupation with translating lost methods of making into contemporary culture and practice. Helix is a product of an ongoing research agenda that centers on volume as an area of architectural exploration.

Helix is a half-scale spiral stair. While the reduced size resolves a number of practical concerns—weight, liability, access—the piece celebrates its impracticality. It is both column and stair, yet hangs from the ceiling. Its uncertainty and altered scale inject playful characteristics into the surrounding space, while maintaining an allegiance to the past and the known.

A second preoccupation of ours is what we term "plastic rhetoric." The solid, heavy, and volumetric action of casting concrete transforms a liquid matter into a solid mass that wants to crack. The stair's plastic and curvaceous treads reflect the material's earlier liquid state. Its twisting accelerates as it wraps around the support column, appearing to replasticize the figure. The entire construct's organic and malleable appearance is counterintuitive in light of the zero tolerance system of nesting and keying from unit to unit.

Spirals are ubiquitous across cultures and times. Helix is our spiral.

1: Mold positive
2: Plywood mother mold
3: Mold assembly

4: Scale prototype

4

5: View inside the BSA Space

6: Detail
7: Column detail
8: Unit key detail
9: Detail drawing

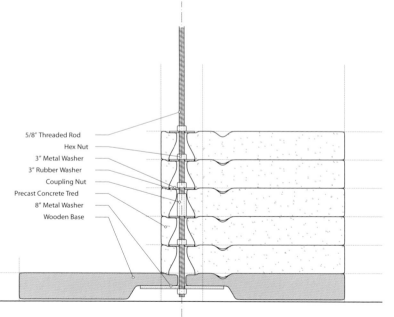

5/8" Threaded Rod
Hex Nut
3" Metal Washer
3" Rubber Washer
Coupling Nut
Precast Concrete Tred
8" Metal Washer
Wooden Base

Cumulus

A Family of Jewelry, 2013

Cumulus is a family of designed objects reminiscent of cloud formations—not only for its rhetorical appearance, but for its capacity to morph, adapt, and change. Clouds are often perceived to carry significance beyond their physical states. While some individual items in the Cumulus family appear familiar as a known type—for instance the pearl—the same system transforms, mutates, multiplies, and evolves into a family of solutions, each producing their own identity within the large family of cloud formations.

    The ring manifestations of Cumulus range from a single pearl ring to volumetric statement pieces. The cufflinks are designed to be pressure fit into a standard buttonhole. The single ball end is just small enough to pass through the hole with a concentrated pressure, but large enough not to come out without directed effort.

1

1: Family portrait

2: Cumulus Ring #504 Demi in sterling silver
3: Cumulus Cufflink #504 Demi

2

3

La Voûte de LeFevre

Banvard Gallery, Knowlton School of Architecture
Columbus, Ohio, 2012

La Voûte de LeFevre is a mashup of ancient stereotomic vault construction with contemporary computation and advanced fabrication. The vault is a compression-only structure calculated through a custom simulation program to determine how large each unit's opening should be in order to adjust its mass in relation to its neighbors. The project employs stereotomy to inform swarf toolpaths that volumetrically and efficiently carve the unique units to align precisely with each other. The purpose of this research is not to revert to an antiquated architecture, but to reengage a problem that may be unfamiliar to contemporary culture. This terrain produces something new, an architecture that is somehow ancient yet contemporary, heavy yet light, familiar yet alien.

1

1: Elevation
2: Interior view

3: Swarf milling
4: Units after carving
5: Tooling
6: Sanding

7: Assembly
8: Unit organization
9: Detail of the back and indexing
10: Assembly

11: View from under the vault
12: Top view
13: Bottom view

14: Details of the column bases
15: Unit volume calculation drawing

14

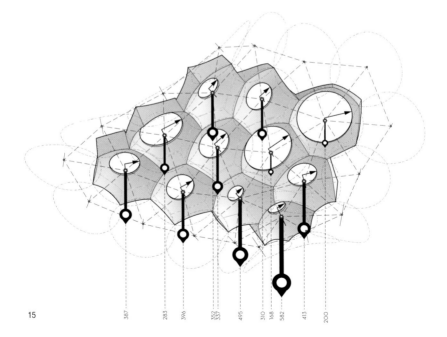

15

387   283   396   352   495   310   582   413   200
              337   168

Pongo

A Coat Rack, 2012

Pongo is a curved translation of the twisted-stick coat rack—forming a continuous, plastic, and voluptuous object of affection. "Belly buttons" occur around holes where bolts can cinch the sticks together. These devices make the assembly process visible, while maintaining an ambiguous impression of fleshlike forms. The three sticks wrap around one another so that the bolts align with the neighboring parts, making assembly a simple task that requires no instructions, while packing nicely for shipping when disassembled.

We feel strongly that great designs appear to be effortless, objects of desire that function while maintaining a state of comfort. Our design methodology translates proven and established classics into contemporary methods of making. This translation serves to invert a new identity to a familiar strategy.

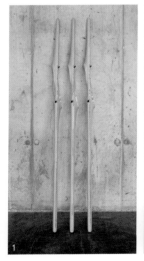
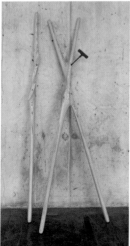

1: Assembly process   2: Pongo (baltic birch plywood)

3: Torso detail (solid ash)

4: 5-axis milling process
5: Assembly process detail

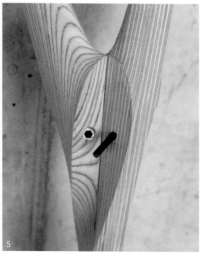

Periscope

Foam Tower, National 10Up! Competition
Atlanta, Georgia, 2010

Periscope is the winning entry of the 10Up! architecture competition: an experiment derived from our ongoing preoccupation with volume. The competition brief was an exercise in constraint. It called for entries that could be constructed in twenty-four hours in a ten-foot by ten-foot plot. No height limit was given. Taking advantage of this oversight, the form of the tower inverts the structural rhetoric of what appears to be a tensile fabric lifted by impossibly thin compression rods. In reality, the sixty-foot tall tower is constructed of expanded polystyrene foam blocks that were robotically cut with a custom hot-wire, stacked, and then placed in compression by tension cables that attach the very large and wind-prone installation to a heavy, stabilizing foundation.

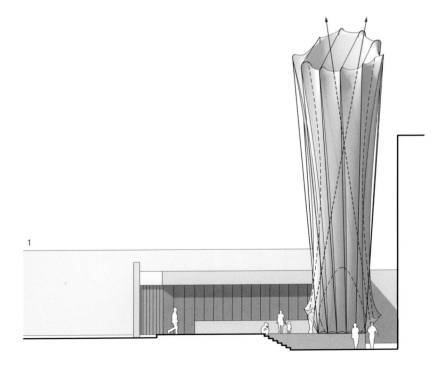

1

1: Elevation

2: Installation

3: Robotic hot-wire carving
4: Crane assembly
5: Assembly
6: Scrap material awaiting recycling

7: Assembly process
8: Detail view
9: Sub-assembly diagram

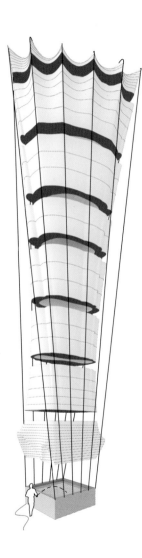

Drawn Dress
Fashioning Digital Fabrication, 2009

For the architect, the digital era has transformed the process of design and fabrication, fueling the fire of rebellion against the standardized construction unit. Today, the architect dreams of efficient transformations, parametric constraints, and developable surfaces, borrowing, oftentimes recklessly, sartorial techniques and language from the fashion industry—darting, draping, patterning. Why then do architects' contemporaries in fashion design still surround themselves with dress forms and work tables? There is a clear disconnect between the methods of working and the moments of progress within the respective fields. The fashion industry is still split between made-to-measure couture and the pret-a-porter S-M-L-XL and numerically coded standardized sizes. When viewed in comparison, the architecture field and the fashion industry have become uniquely successful at processes that the alternate field struggles to get right. This potential synergy is seemingly apparent and useful; however, little interaction occurs at the pedagogical level beyond superficial discussions and conceptual leaps. As architects take this opportunity to reflect on how the digital process has affected their practice, we have the opportunity to engage a similar process that has yet to take the digital leap.

Charged with the task of designing, developing, and constructing a digitally drawn dress, this comparative process serves as a catalyst to rarify architecture's contribution in the digital era. While it is easy to assume technology as advanced, this process illustrated the purpose behind the division of these two fields. These dresses are naughty. No seam is straight. Each seam is a three-dimensional curve, a product of our dedication to digital complexity, making the dresses difficult to sew. This critical process embraces reciprocity between drawing and construction and by doing so, pushes processes beyond the sequences found in the currently divided fields of architecture and fashion.

Hoop Dress

MARC FORNES / THEVERYMANY

Marc Fornes

74   **Plasti(k) Pavilion**
76   **non Lin / Lin Pavilion**
80   **Y / Surf / Struc**
84   **Labrys Frisae**
88   **Chromatae**
90   **Double Agent White**
94   **Louis Vuitton—Yayoi Kusama**

MARC FORNES / THEVERYMANY is a Brooklyn-based architecture studio committed to the design and construction of *prototypical architecture* via custom computational methods. The practice is structured through the process of rigorous serial experimentation. This methodology delineates a research trajectory of continuously developable processes with internal differentiation per project through case-specific constraints and conditions. Thus, the body of work becomes a continuous investigation, with intensive focus on architecture's relation to structure, form description, information modeling, and digital fabrication.

Form description explores the means through which a single overall geometry is segmented into multiple sub-elements. *Information modeling* is the means through which logistical information is integrated into computational models. *Digital fabrication* pushes toward seamless modes of translation from file to physical form.

The experimentation incorporates *explicit and encoded* parameters through which the research methodology is recursively refined. This process requires the explicit description of a given phenomenon be made into a series of discrete steps, forming a hierarchically ordered set of basic logical operations, or *protocol*. Through encoding, these ordered protocols are translated into syntax executable by a computer. The control made possible by these processes allows the research to be continually informed by prior investigations.

The desire is not to generate models, nor installations, but rather 1:1 scale structures, prototypical architectures. The methodology continually pushes constraints at larger scales to engage fundamental questions of stability, working to advance formal complexity and structural efficiency simultaneously. The construction of a prototype is the construction of a system *in formation*, continually developing toward architecture.

Design and research through built prototypes establishes a feedback loop between the digital and physical domains. At work is the implementation of custom computational techniques to interrogate the physical ramifications of digital design. The effect is an atmosphere of rich formal interplay and perceptual complexity driven by an attitude of rigorous exploration.

Plasti(k) Pavilion
Semipermanent Folly within a Public Park
Washington University, St. Louis, Missouri, 2011

How can space be defined with the least amount of unique parts?

Plasti(k) Pavilion investigates the production of architectural space through approximation: a highly defined NURBS surface through a 3-D Aperiodic Packing (a minimum of unique primitives and maximum display of diversity). This creates a gain of *definition* via a loss of *resolution*.

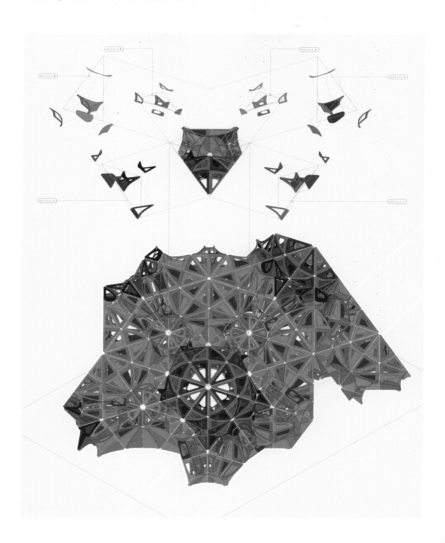

non Lin / Lin Pavilion
Permanent Collection
FRAC Centre, Orleans, France, 2011

Could a nonlinear network morphology generate an overall surface condition?

non Lin / Lin Pavilion is an unprecedented prototypical architecture exploring the dramatic change of morphology. Derived from the geometric attributes of the branch, or "Y," the computational protocol generates architectural space through the relationship of network to surface.

Structural networks open up and recombine to create a comprehensive surface condition, producing a spatial experience by the most fundamental definitive means: enclosure. The pavilion is therefore an investigation in describing unprecedented spatial organizations through conventional materials and modes of fabrication.

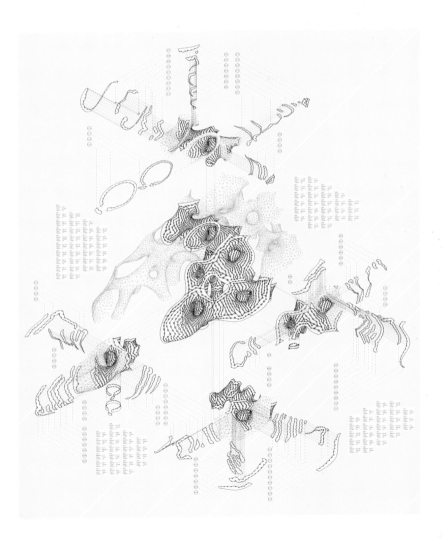

Y / Surf / Struc

Permanent Collection
Centre Pompidou, Paris, 2011–present

Could a surface evolve into a distributed network morphology?

Y / Surf / Struc constitutes a radical change of morphology: the prototype explores the transition from surface (the minimum definition of space/enclosure) to a distributed network (structure). The resulting geometry is described through a system of agents with schizophrenic behavior.

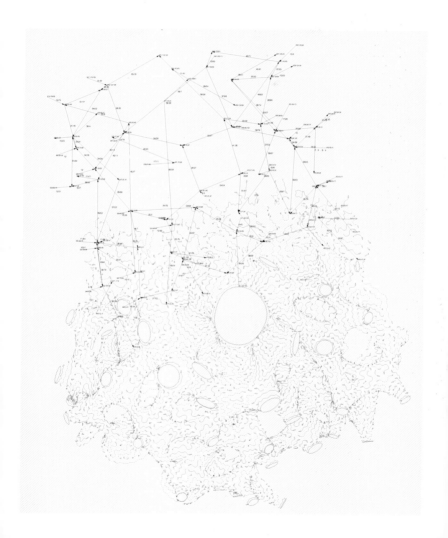

In order to define all cases present, the behaviors must conflict and compete. Y / Surf / Struc defies classic modes of descriptive geometry, investigating localized protocols of search via distributed and competitive agents (encapsulated sets of computational rules), able to account for a broad range of curvature issues and formal conditions.

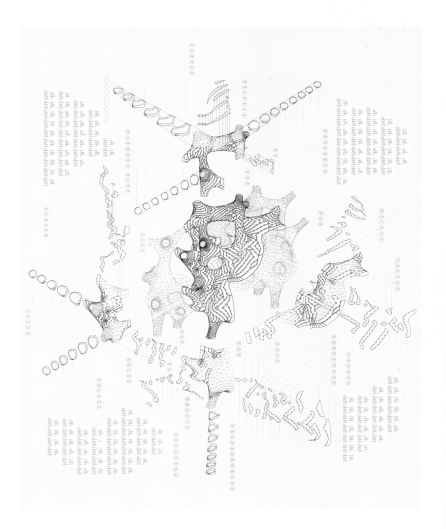

Labrys Frisae
Semipermanent Installation
Graffiti Gone Global, Art Basel Miami Beach, Miami, Florida, 2011–present

Could a volume dissolve into a distributed network morphology?

Labrys Frisae explores the reciprocal relationship of surface and network at an inhabitable scale. The project furthers the research trajectory through the negotiation between an increase of scale and the resulting logistics and social-assembly management.

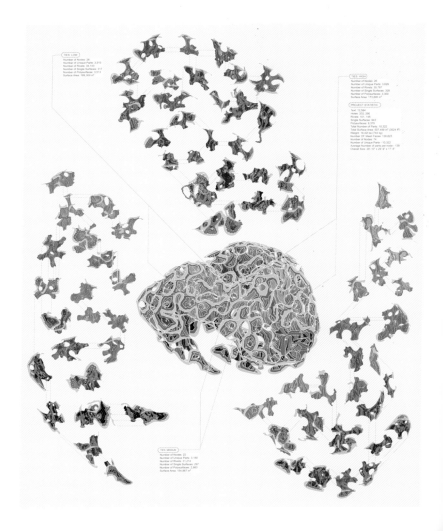

Labrys Frisae engages self-supported structures through high degrees of internal double curvature. The resulting morphology, between surface and network, defines interior as well as exterior envelopes.

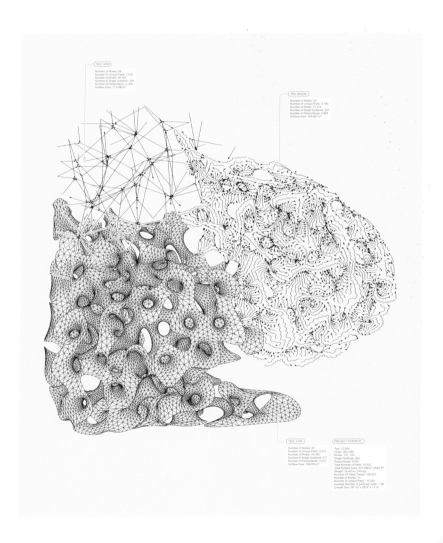

Chromatae

Public Art

Denver Botanic Garden, Denver, Colorado, 2012

How could computational coloring intensify geometry into a lush sensory environment?

Chromatae explores the production of immersive formal and chromatic environments through custom computational protocols. Multiple skin descriptions, from Cheshire *modulo* bands to nonlinear gradients, are applied to a single continuous morphology, enlivening the spatial experience.

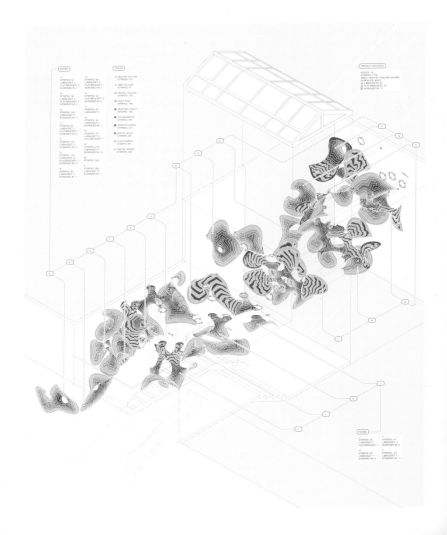

Double Agent White

Permanent Collection of the Centre National des Arts Plastiques
Atelier Calder, Sache, France, 2012

How can a structural skin synthesize assembly and translate efficiency into a spatial experience?

At the boundary between art and architecture, Double Agent White must satisfy constraints of enclosure, experience, and portability. The structural skin is optimized through a dual set of descriptions correlating to assembly and porosity.

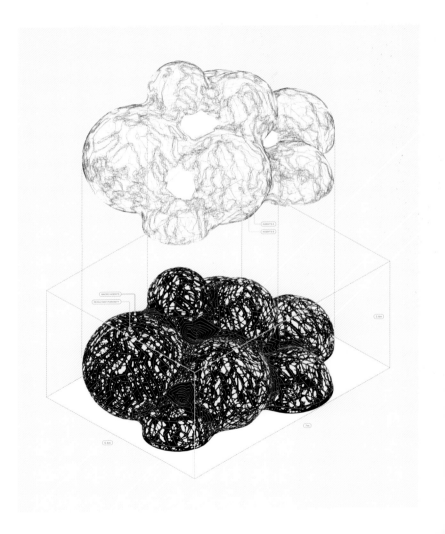

A first system of macro-agents strives toward minimum parts for assembly and maximum length to fit within a small transportation case. A secondary system overlaps for maximum intricacy of aperture and transversal structural connections.

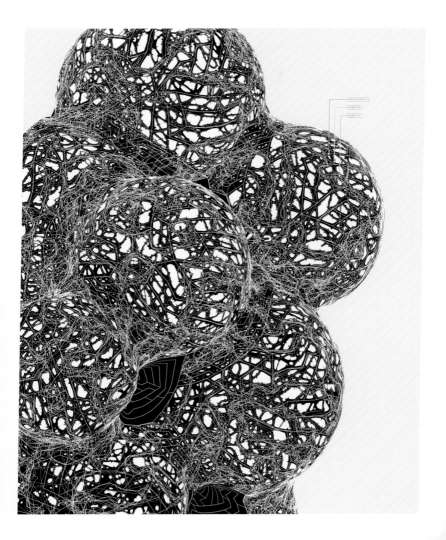

Louis Vuitton—Yayoi Kusama
Pop-up Store
Selfridges, London, 2012

Can carbon fiber be developed for the production of economically viable architecture?

THEVERYMANY's development for Louis Vuitton's Selfridges store demonstrates the design and production of the first all-carbon fiber structural skins applied to architecture. The project integrates issues of form and materiality into an ultra-thin and lightweight structure.

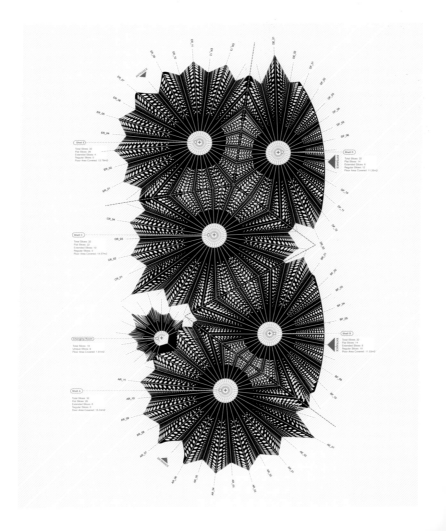

The project follows ongoing research that investigates structural forms through compound curvature. The segments, each unique in pattern and modular in shape, are industrially produced from large reinforced carbon fiber sheets that are flat and vacuum-infused, therefore low cost. Kusama's pattern is laser cut into unrolled *patron* shapes, placed onto a temporary foam scaffold (as opposed to wet-laid onto expensive molds), and structurally bound, allowing for integration of electrical networks within the pleats.

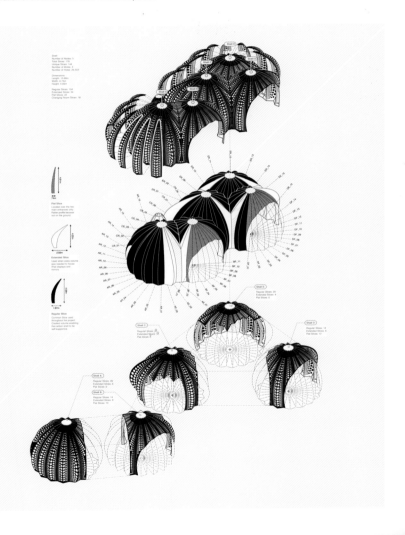

PRAUD

Rafael Luna and Dongwoo Yim

100 **PRAUD Range**
102 **I Want to be METROPOLITAN**
104 **Casa Periscopio**
108 **Leaning House**
112 **Topology and Typology**
114 **Helsinki Public Library**
118 **Busan Opera House**
120 **Hotel Liesma**
122 **Seattle Jelly Bean**

It is not easy to define the profession of architecture with a single sentence. Sometimes an architect is understood as a designer, and sometimes as a consultant. Some architects focus on a specific scale, while others focus on specific programs for projects. However, the *range* of an architect is not subjected to scale or program, but rather related to the different *roles* of an architect. As young architects, we set up a range of roles that we believe we can and should address in order to develop a holistic understanding of our career. We rearranged our projects to understand the four major architects' roles that we think are relevant to construct our identity and personality: architect as dreamer, practitioner, researcher, and theorist.

Dreamer: Sometimes, an architect has to be a dreamer who can propose a vision that is rather futuristic, or unrealistic at the moment, in order to address a social demand and advances in technology to induce a paradigm shift.

Practitioner: An architect takes the role of master builder with the pursuit of executing a design intention, while addressing construction methods and technology. An architect should be aware of local construction materials, methods, and cultures when he / she develops the design phase.

Researcher: Aside from designing a building, an architect needs to construct paradigms and perspectives on urbanism. This can be developed through research on cities at various scales and shared with others in order to engage a dialogue.

Theorist: Sometimes young architects tend to lose their theoretical background once they start their own practice. However, developing your thesis and solidifying your discourse is extremely important when you want to position your projects within a lineage of architectural history and theory.

PRAUD Range

Parsons The New School for Design
New York, New York, 2013

In the Range exhibition, PRAUD mapped out all of the projects to show the range of our works as well as the range of architects' roles. As the name PRAUD (Progressive Research, Architecture, Urbanism, and Design) indicates, we laid out the projects by the types of works we do to present how PRAUD is structured and which areas we are focused on. The projects are also arranged by the roles of the architect as a dreamer, practitioner, researcher, and theorist.

It is very important to present all of our works as one single map, instead of just showing some outstanding ones, and to interrelate each project to the other to share the idea and the structure of our works. Therefore, the exhibition is not focusing on presenting projects, but rather focusing on the way we have been developing our own identity and where we are headed.

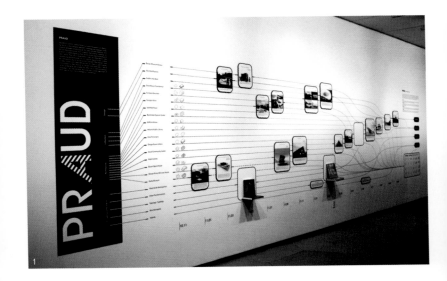

1: View of installation

2: View of installation (detail)
3: Exhibition drawing

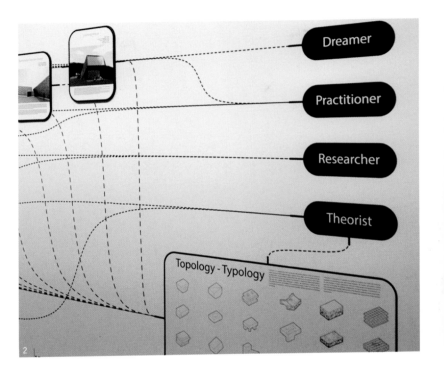

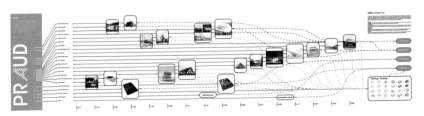

I Want to Be Metropolitan

ORO Editions, 2012

I Want to Be Metropolitan is a research effort on the mini metropolis, using Boston as a case study to provide a different reading of the city. The study focuses on showing the efforts that the city of Boston has made in order to grow with metropolitan characteristics while remaining at a much smaller scale than cities like New York, London, or Tokyo. The morphology of Boston has been achieved through different metropolitan interventions that occur at different scales. These are divided at an infrastructural scale, urban scale, and architectural scale. By means of analyzing these different aspects, we can compose a vision of a future Boston, or Fictitious Boston, derived from its metropolitan potential.

The book is structured into four chapters addressing the different scales of analysis. The first chapter compiles general data of the city and provides a background view of the infrastructural efforts that the city has made to accommodate its population. The second chapter identifies Boston's poly-centrality, a characteristic that appears in big metropolitan cities like Tokyo. In homage to *Made in Tokyo*, chapter three catalogs hybrid buildings in Boston, referencing the ambiguity of these buildings being born out of a metropolitan context and transported to a less dense setting. Chapter four concludes the study by introducing our vision of new projects for the city of Boston to generate an open conversation about the topic. This leads us to the possible implementation of the research topic and methodology on other cities similar in size and pace to Boston.

Present-day urban topics and strategies mainly focus on cities with extreme conditions such as high density, increasing congestion, and fast growth. This book intends to create a dialogue that addresses the missing topics in urbanism for smaller, slower, and much more stable cities, the mini metropolis.

1: Cover
2–6: Interior spreads

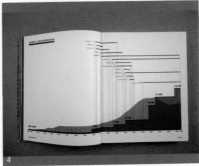

Casa Periscopio
Costa del Sol, El Salvador, 2012

Located within an enclosed beach community on the Pacific coast of El Salvador, this house aims to interact with nature as an artifact, while addressing local means of construction in order to achieve a new language. The most popular construction method in El Salvador is the concrete-block masonry system, which allows for walls to act as structural components. Therefore, we tackled the task of creating an open space that has a duality between the interior and exterior by dividing the topology into three masses and stairs, treating them as structural components that can hold each other. An overhanging mass on top holds the private rooms, a smaller mass at one corner on the ground floor holds the kitchen, a linear mass stabilizes the top mass, and a staircase at the other corner helps the top mass levitate over the living room. This stacking system is to maximize the advantage of the construction method.

For this the tropical climate, the hanging mass is extended toward the ocean not only to frame the view of the ocean but also to shade the living room. The central void is planned to give more natural air circulation that can flow throughout the whole house from the first-floor open living room to the second floor, where most of the bedrooms are located.

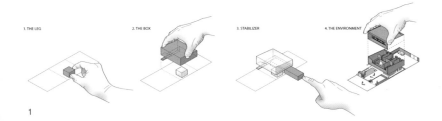

1. THE LEG   2. THE BOX   3. STABILIZER   4. THE ENVIRONMENT

1

1: Process diagram

2: View from the west
3–4: Section drawings

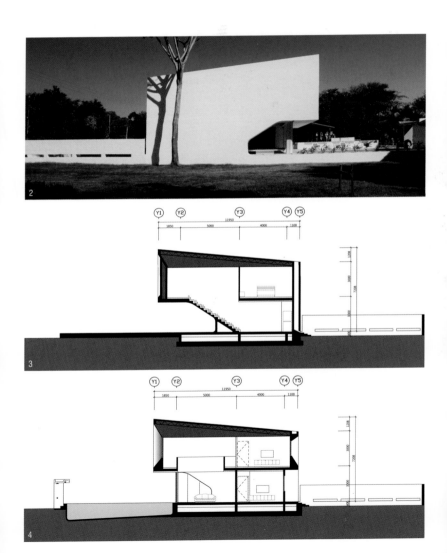

5: View from the south
6: View from entrance

7: Dining room
8: View from living room to pool
9: Floorplans

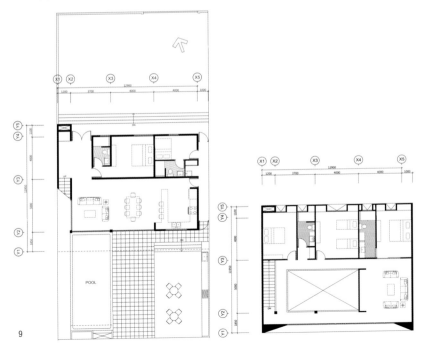

9

Leaning House
Chungpyong, South Korea, 2013

Because of size and budget constraints, this single-family house project relied on a simple massing logic. The massing concept employs two boxes: one standing straight and another box leaning against it. The intention was to create a fluid space inside the leaning box so that all the rooms of the weekend house are visually and physically connected as one space.

The leaning system naturally became the spatial concept for this project. The leaning box sits on the ground at one end while the smaller box offers structural support for the other end. In order to explore this spatial relation, we used reinforced concrete as the local means of construction, in order to create a structural diagonal box that could hold the rooms while in cantilever. This logic allows for an efficiency within the system with no need for additional structural elements.

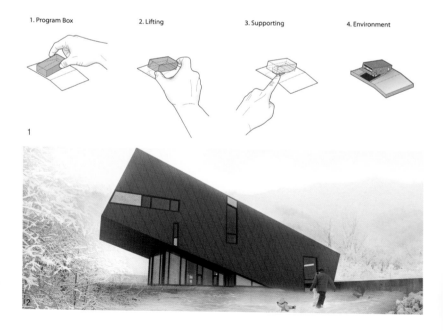

1. Program Box   2. Lifting   3. Supporting   4. Environment

1

2

1: Process diagram
2: Rendering of view from neighborhood

3–4: Section drawings

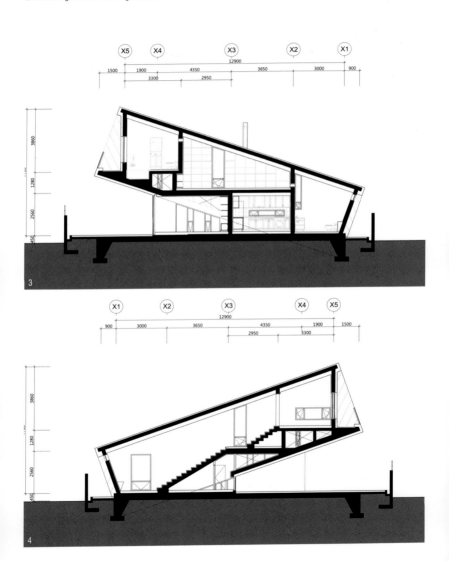

5: Floor plans

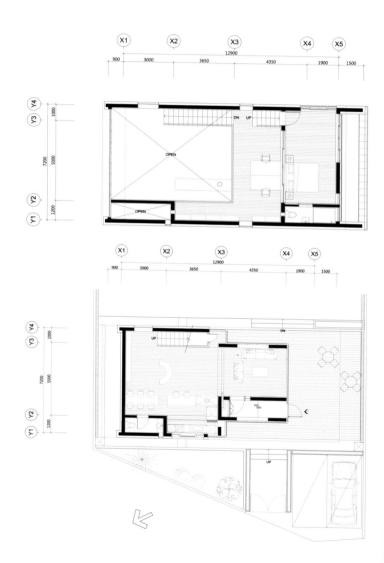

6–14: Construction photos
15: Rendering of view from street

Topology and Typology
Elective Seminar, Rhode Island School of Design, 2011–2012

What is contemporary architecture? The word *contemporary* means something that exists in the present. In many cases, apart from the architectural field, *contemporary* is used as a synonym for *modern*. However, in architecture, *modernism* defines the specific language of a building, not limited to architecture that was built in the modern period. In the same manner, *contemporarism* can be defined as an architectural vocabulary, rather than just a chronology. How, then, can we define contemporary architecture? If we define it in a chronological way, any project that is built in the present will be considered contemporary architecture, but will no longer be such after time passes. There is no longer a taxonomy in architecture because anything that is built in the present just becomes contemporary architecture. However, just as we define modernism, perhaps there is a way of defining contemporarism based on architectural vocabulary.

Topology and *Typology* are part of an architectural vocabulary that PRAUD pursues to address these questions. If we can define contemporarism as an architectural language, what type of architecture can be categorized as such?

Topology is a mathematical term concerned with spatial properties that are preserved under continuous deformations of objects. This concept can be easily adopted in architecture to explain the relationship between solid and void, architecture and urban, presence and absence. The relationship is defined by the three-dimensional form of a building, not by geometrical shapes in plan. This is a key feature in contemporary architecture that relies on the third typology that Anthony Vidler defined as the relation between architectural form and the city context.

Typology is an architectural system that breaks the modernist paradigms by generating a new systematic language. PRAUD explores new strategies of space manipulation that have broken modernist tendencies. We rely on the first and second typologies, based on Vidler's perspective, that address components of architecture and system. In Typology, we challenge the conventional concept of architectural components and systems, such as the Domino System, in order to go beyond modernism to define contemporarism.

PRAUD seeks harmony between Topology and Typology that addresses contemporarism in both architectural form and system. It is a way of developing an integrated totalitarian architecture from the form of architecture to the system of it, and this is what PRAUD believes the contemporary to be.

1: Topology models
2: Typology models
3: Hybrid typology

Modernism

Horizontal Core

Slab Manipulation

Structural Pattern

Structural Displacement

3D Pattern

Stacking

Single Surface

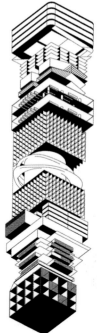

2

3

Helsinki Public Library
Helsinki, Finland, 2012

This project shows how *Topology* and *Typology* can be harmonized to form architectural space. Though the site is surrounded by medium-rise buildings, the required program area is not enough to have the library meet the neighborhood building-height restrictions. Therefore, the programmed mass is folded to meet the surrounding context height. As it folds, it creates a cantilevered part on both sides, which is held by a top mass that holds the tensile stress. Therefore, an inverted doughnut pyramid became the topology of the library. This doughnut form provides a unique third space that is additional to the required program. It is an urban-scale public space inside the library that is created by the natural void of the topology.

In terms of typology, aside from the top tensile plate, we introduced horizontal tubes to hold the lateral force of the building. The library has two major truss systems at both sides of the building to hold the majority of the structural stress, and there should be members that hold lateral force. These horizontal tubes are also related to programmed rooms that need the least natural light. The typology system becomes not only structural but a spatial organizing system as well.

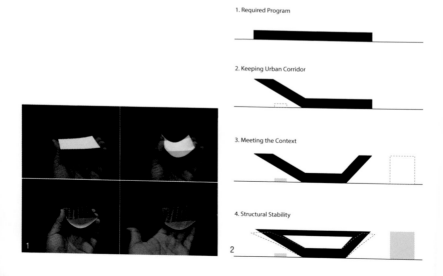

1. Required Program

2. Keeping Urban Corridor

3. Meeting the Context

4. Structural Stability

1

2

1: Concept model
2: Process diagram

3: Rendering of aerial view
4: Rendering of view from park

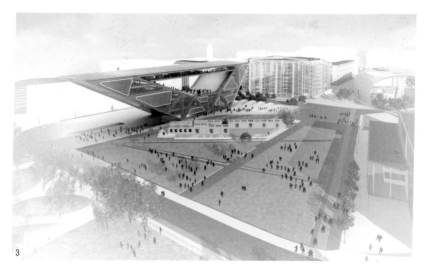

3

4

5–6: Day and night views from park
7: Exploded diagram

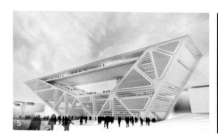

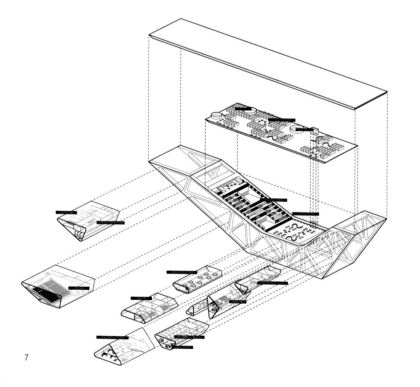

7

8: Rendering of urban living room
9: Rendering of lobby
10: Section

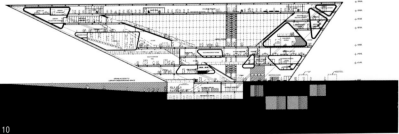

Busan Opera House

Busan, South Korea, 2011

The concept starts from reevaluating how multiple performance facilities can share common stage and chamber facilities. Therefore, the basic topology of the project became *stacking*, similar to a pebble tower on the beach, where we pile one theater over another.

To achieve this goal, we developed a transformable "cylinder" not only for stage and chamber functions but also for structural stability. Multiple disks in the cylinder can move vertically depending on the type and size needed for a performance and number of simultaneous performances. This vertical movement also creates voids that provide visual connection between floors and masses so that a performance can be shown to audiences in various ways. These disks can also rotate so that a performance can happen in multiple directions as well.

The cylinder in the middle is one of the major structural systems of the building. However, we needed to develop an intelligent typology to create a generous and flexible space inside. The typological system used is analogous to a coiled hose. We adopted this idea and designed a tube structure at the periphery that wraps around each "pebble," giving it structural strength and a solid form.

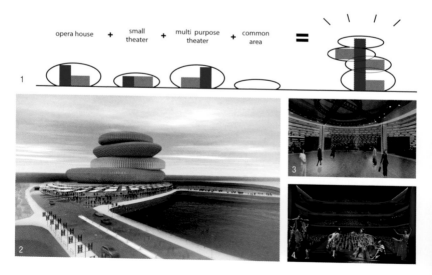

1: Process diagram
2: Rendering of view from city
3: Rendering of opera stage
4: Rendering of stage

5: Rendering of view from sea
6: Transforming cylinder diagrams

5

6

Hotel Liesma
Liesma, Latvia, 2011

Sitting by the shore of the Baltic Sea, this hotel project called for an expansion of the program, with additional rooms and public facilities. As it is deprived from some of the best views toward the sea because of a dense forest area between the hotel and the beach, we wanted to provide a solution through the topology of the project. We conceived having a single mat of rooms that is raised above the tree line. As the mat-type mass is angled, each guest room has a direct view to the sea. Elevating this mass also made it possible to open the ground level to the public, which is covered by the flying mass, so that the space can be used for major public events. In many cases, exploring topology provides a third space that perhaps is not a required program but is needed for the urban context.

The typology required us to deal with issues of supporting the elevated mass of guest rooms as well as its long span. Structural cones that contain the common public facilities are used to hold the vertical load of the flying mass. Aside from these vertical supports, a creative typology was proposed to have long spans of the flying mass: a Vierendeel truss has thicker members than a regular truss system, allowing for a program to fit within the truss. Series of trusses that contain guest rooms are laid out next to each other and linked back to the vertical cones at each node. This creates the uniform floating mass that oversees the Baltic Sea.

1

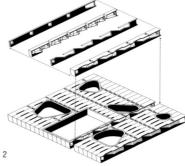

2

1: Rendering of aerial view
2: Typology diagram

3: Rendering of view from forest
4–5: Renderings of views from guest rooms
6–7: Sections

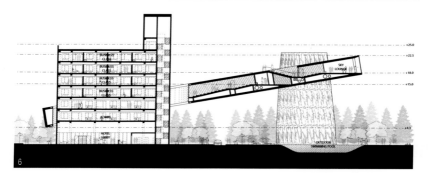

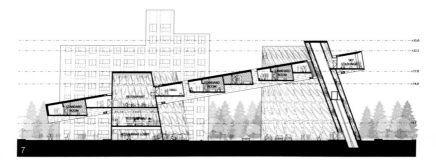

Seattle Jelly Bean
Finalist
Seattle, Washington, 2012

As a dreamer, the architect has a very important role of proposing visionary ideas to the world. It is necessary to construct visions for future culture, technology, and social demands. This may be unrealistic or futuristic, but it speaks of a present need and foresees potential solutions.

PRAUD envisioned the Seattle Jelly Bean project as dreamers rather than as practitioners. Aside from the ground level landscape design that has more attachment to daily uses, the floating "jelly bean" provides new ways for the city to interact with the public. The idea may seem unreasonable, unrealistic, and unbuildable, but the more important thing is to envision the possibilities that this new urban artifact can offer by creating new events, an ever-changing urban space, and a platform for interaction. We consider Seattle to be a mini metropolis and foresee its growth and expansion, which is why we believe that a new icon that celebrates its innovation is necessary to promote the city for the next fifty years.

1

1: Rendering of view from civic center

2: Rendering of view from under the pod
3–6: Renderings during various weather conditions
7: Rendering of a concert beneath the pod

SJET

Skylar J. E. Tibbits

126   **Fluid Crystallization**
128   **BioMolecular Self-Assembly**
132   **Self-Assembly Line**
136   **Logic Matter**
142   **MacroBot and DeciBot**
144   **Self-Folding Structures**
148   **4D Printing: Multi-Material Shape Change**

Across scales, disciplines, materials, methods, and tools, this research-based practice is at the intersection of many worlds. Operating as an architect, artist, designer, and computer scientist based at MIT, Skylar J. E. Tibbits aims to develop self-assembly technologies and programmable materials to reinvent new methods of making at this intersection. Self-assembly is one of the only known phenomena that naturally occurs at every scale, within every discipline, and throughout both biological and synthetic realms. By its very nature, this course of study cannot be defined by traditional domains.

This research began with a question: how can we program physical materials with enough assembly information to enable self-construction and reconfigurability? This research has traversed the worlds of computer science and artificial intelligence, programmable matter, reconfigurable robotics, and Life Sciences. Working closely with experts in every one of these fields, the topic of macro self-assembly has struck a chord and enabled unprecedented collaborations across disciplines, scales, and material toolsets. It is truly a new language of making that now enables complete control and programmability through nearly every material. This revolution is producing shape change, property change, self-construction, computational materials, and replication or evolution of nonbiological material.

Working with a range of industry and government partners, Tibbits develops projects that investigate nanoscale self-assembly of three-dimensional shapes, reconfigurable materials, adaptive products, self-repairing materials, four-dimensional printing technologies (three-dimensional printing plus multi-material shape change), educational toys/devices, adaptive infrastructure (such as water-pipes that adapt to demands), new methods of manufacturing, self-construction scenarios, and reconfigurable space structures. In order to operate at these dynamic extremes he operates simultaneously as researcher, designer, academic, and entrepreneur. For Tibbits, as the silos of knowledge blend, innovation arises and the most interesting developments are produced at the intersection of scalar limits and disciplinary boundaries. This practice is comfortable oscillating between investigating the future while simultaneously developing technologies that have the opportunity to influence tomorrow's built environment.

Skylar Tibbits's work thrives on the endless search for more and occupying this range of the unknown.

Fluid Crystallization

Parsons the New School for Design
New York, New York, 2013

The Fluid Crystallization project investigates hierarchical and nondeterministic self-assembly with large numbers of parts in a fluid medium. Three hundred fifty hollow spheres have been submerged in two hundred gallons of water in a glass tank. Armatures, modeled after carbon atoms, follow intramolecular covalent bonding geometries within atoms. Intermolecular structures are formed as spheres interact with one another in one-, two-, or three-dimensional patterns. The highly dynamic self-assembly characteristic of the system offers a glimpse at material phase change between crystalline solid, liquid, and gaseous states. Turbulence in the water introduces stochastic energy into the system, increasing the entropy and allowing structures to self-assemble, thus transitioning between gas, liquid, and solid phases. Polymorphism may be observed where the same intramolecular structures can solidify in more than one crystalline form, demonstrating the versatile nature of carbon as a building block for life.

In collaboration with: Arthur Olson, Scripps Research Institute; Graham Francis, Marianna Gonzalez, Amir Soltanian, Monica Zhou, and Veronica Emig

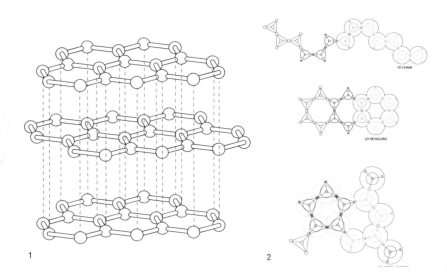

1

2

1: Graphite and Diamond: Carbon-based 2-D and 3-D molecular structures

2: 1-D, 2-D, and 3-D carbon-based structures that can self-organize in the tank

3: Internal armatures and tetrahedral structure of spheres

4: Various components of the spheres and internal armatures for neutral buoyancy

5: 200-gallon tank and 350 self-organizing neutrally buoyant spheres in the Range exhibition

3

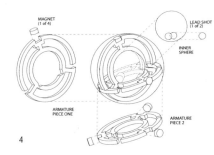

4

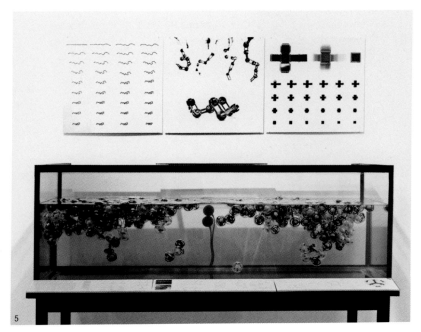

5

Bio-Molecular Self-Assembly

TEDGlobal, Edinburgh, Scotland, 2012, and
Autodesk University, Las Vegas, Nevada, 2012

The Bio-Molecular Self-Assembly project was exhibited at the 2012 TEDGlobal
Conference in Edinburgh, Scotland. Participants of TEDGlobal each received a
unique glass flask containing anywhere from four to twelve red, black, or white parts.
When the glass flask was shaken randomly, the independent parts found each other
and self-assembled into various molecular structures. The flasks contained a custom
tag that identified the type of molecular structure and the ingredients for successful
self-assembly.

Self-assembly is the process by which a system spontaneously assembles
from discrete components without external guidance. For successful self-assembly to
take place, three things are required: geometry, energy, and attraction—all of which,
in theory, can occur at many different scales.

In collaboration with: Arthur Olson, Scripps Research Institute; and Carlos
Olguin, Autodesk, Inc.

1

1: Various plastic dodecahedron structures ready to be placed inside of the glass flasks for self-assembly

2: Necessary ingredients for self-assembly

3: Five hundred glass flasks with various components and colors to demonstrate self-assembly of precise Bio-Molecular structures

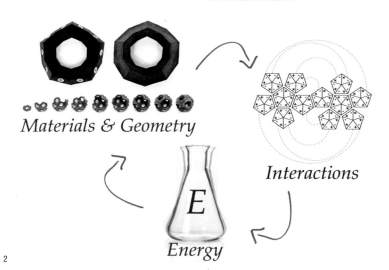

Materials & Geometry

Interactions

E

Energy

2

3

4: Self-assembly process of a tobacco plant virus
in a glass flask
5: Chiral self-assembly: the process of self-sorting
right-handed and left-handed structures

4

5

6: Three tags with information and images of the
Bio-Molecular structures for the self-assembly exhibit

Tobacco Plant Virus
Assembly model based on research performed by
Skylar Tibbits of MIT and Arthur Olson of the Scripps
Research Institute in association with Autodesk
Research.

For additional information, please visit:
www.bioselfassembly.net

BIO-MOLECULAR
SELF-ASSEMBLY

NUMBER:

TEDGLOBAL 2012

Autodesk

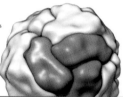

Ferritin Protein Assembly
Assembly model based on research performed by
Skylar Tibbits of MIT and Arthur Olson of the Scripps
Research Institute in association with Autodesk
Research.

For additional information, please visit:
www.bioselfassembly.net

BIO-MOLECULAR
SELF-ASSEMBLY

NUMBER:

TEDGLOBAL 2012

Autodesk

Catechol Dioxygenase Enzyme
Assembly model based upon research performed by
Skylar Tibbits of MIT and Arthur Olson of the Scripps
Research Institute. Produced by Science Within
Reach in association with Autodesk.

For additional information, please visit:
www.bioselfassembly.net

BIO-MOLECULAR
SELF-ASSEMBLY

NUMBER:

TEDGLOBAL 2012

Autodesk

6

Self-Assembly Line
TED Long Beach
Long Beach, California, 2012

The Self-Assembly Line project was exhibited at TED Long Beach in 2012. This project is a large-scale implementation of a self-assembly virus capsid, demonstrated as an interactive and performative structure. A discrete set of modules is activated by the rotation of a large container that forces interaction between units. The unit geometry and attraction mechanisms ensure the units will come into contact with one another and auto-align into locally-correct configurations. Over time as more units come into contact, break away, and reconnect, larger furniture-scale elements emerge. Given different sets of unit geometries and attraction polarities various structures could be achieved. By changing the external conditions, the geometry of the unit, the attraction of the units, and the number of units supplied, the desired global configuration can be programmed.

In collaboration with: Arthur Olson, Scripps Research Institute; Adam Bly, SEED Media Group; Martin Seymour, Andrew Manto, Erioseto Hendranata, Justin Gallagher, Laura Salazar, Veronica Emig, and Aaron Olson

1

1: The self-assembly process from twelve individual units into a precise dodecahedron structure

2: A large rotating chamber and self-assembly units form a dodecahedron structure.

3: Two of the foam-based pentamer units for self-assembly structures

3

4: Detail of connections on the self-assembly chamber

5–6: Night view of the static Self-Assembly Line structure
and dodecahedrons

Logic Matter

Massachusetts Institute of Technology
Cambridge, Massachusetts, 2010

Logic Matter is a system of passive, mechanical, digital logic modules that enable self-guided assembly of large-scale structures. As opposed to current systems in self-reconfigurable robotics or programmable matter, Logic Matter introduces scalability, robustness, redundancy, and local heuristics to achieve passive assembly and material decision-making. The geometry and interaction of the modules implement the digital NAND (Negated AND) logic gate, demonstrating physical computation with digital/physical information. The physical prototype successfully demonstrates the described mechanics, encoded information, and passive self-guided assembly. There are wide applications for computational and programmable materials from information-rich construction, reconfigurable material optimization, material hard drives, and three-dimensional circuit assembly.

Advisors: Terry Knight, Architecture, MIT; Patrick Winston, Electrical Engineering & Computer Science (EECS), MIT; and Erik Demaine, EECS, MIT

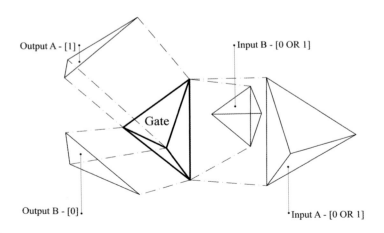

1: Diagrammatic relationship between geometry and input orientation, with two outputs representing the NAND digital logic gate

2: Logic Matter units connect into a linear chain that bends in three dimensions based on an oscillating input sequence.

3: Logic Matter units forming a linear chain

2

3

4: The input sequence of 1 and 1 results in the spatial
output "down," representing a 0.
5: Diagrams of a single-path "random walk" on the
exterior of a sphere

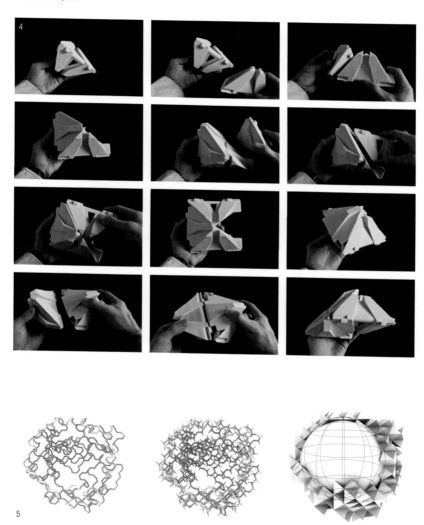

6: The input sequence of 0 and 0 results in the spatial
output "up," representing a 1.

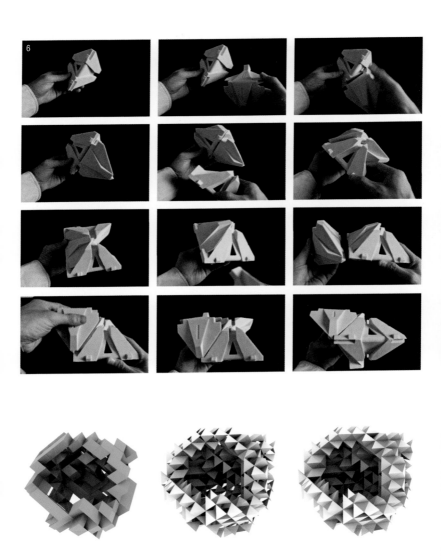

7: The assembly process of Logic Matter units connecting into a linear chain based on an oscillating input sequence of 0's and 1's.

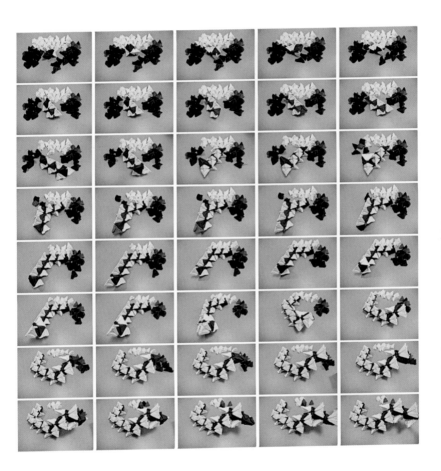

MacroBot and DeciBot

Massachusetts Institute of Technology
Cambridge, Massachusetts, 2009

The MacroBot and DeciBot projects were presented in the Programmable Matter program at InfoChemistry, a conference organized by the Defense Advanced Research Project Agency (DARPA) in 2009. The DeciBot is part of the larger *bot family of programmable matter one-dimensional folding chains. The *bot family contains reconfigurable robotic systems at nanometer, millimeter, centimeter, and decimeter part lengths. The MacroBot and DeciBot are the largest of the family with overall dimensions of 144 by 18 by 18 inches unfolded and 36 by 36 by 36 inches folded into a cube. The reconfigurable chains can be programmed to change shape from any one arbitrary structure into any other by communicating with each node and interpolating between positions.

In collaboration with: Neil Gershenfeld, The Center for Bits and Atoms, and MIT

1–2: The large-scale, single-strand reconfigurable robot with connected units can transform from any 1-D, 2-D, or 3-D structure.

3: The programmed transformation of a single strand into a 1-D, 2-D, and 3-D structure over time

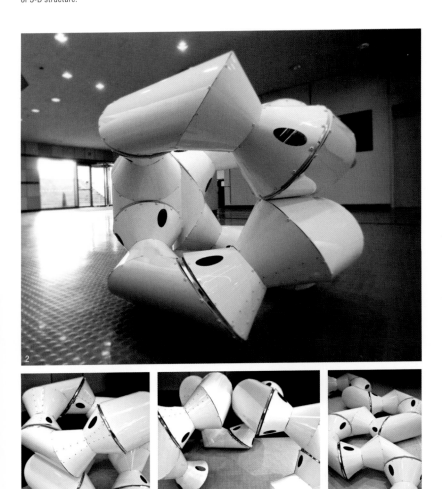

Self-Folding Structures

Massachusetts Institute of Technology
Cambridge, Massachusetts, 2012

The Self-Folding Structures are a series of projects investigating passive reconfigurability and programmable materials. The self-folding protein is a single strand of material with embedded fold-angles that, when thrown into the air, self-assemble into the three-dimensional structure of the desired protein. This project aims to study folding macro-scale proteins to gain insight into nonintuitive and intangible aspects of self-assembly phenomena. The Crambin protein has been utilized due to its well-studied characteristics and minimal size. This technology appears to be scalable to larger protein strands and other one-dimensional to three-dimensional self-assembly systems.

The Biased Chains and Biased Planes projects demonstrate similar one-dimensional and two-dimensional reconfigurability with passive systems that transform from flexible materials into rigid three-dimensional structures. The chains are activated with random shaking, while the planes contain potential energy and are released simply by subtle movement.

In collaboration with: Arthur Olson, Scripps Research Institute; and Noa Flaherty and Candace Chen, MIT

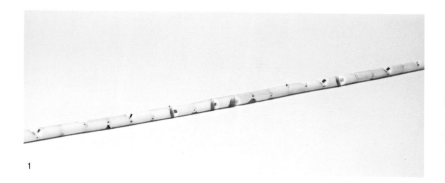

1

1–7: A single strand self-folds into the complex 3-D
structure of the Crambin protein.

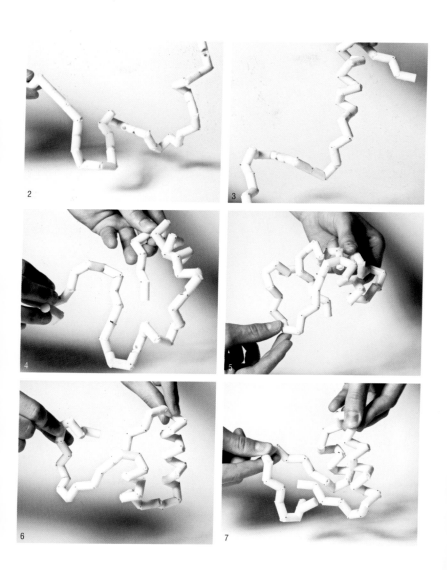

8: Identical separate units can be connected in various orientations to "program" the chain.
9: A rigid 3-D structure, programmed and self-assembled into the final form

10: The random shaking process and transformation of the Biased Chains from a flexible strand into a rigid 3-D structure

8

9

11: The final rigid 3-D structure of a hyperbolic paraboloid, self-folded from a flat sheet

12: The 2-D sheet with geometric information and embedded potential energy, ready for self-folding into the final 3-D structure

11

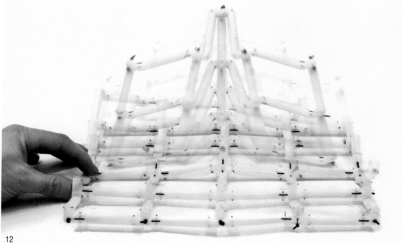

12

4-D Printing: Multi-Material Shape Change

TED Long Beach
Long Beach, California, 2013

4-D Printing is a collaboration between the education and research and development departments at Stratasys and MIT's Self-Assembly Lab, and was presented at TED Long Beach in 2013. This new process demonstrates a radical shift in rapid-prototyping with multi-material prints provided by Connex Technology and the added capability of complete transformation from one shape to another, directly off the print-bed. This means that parts can be printed to independently change shape and material properties when submerged in water. This technique offers a streamlined path from idea to reality with full functionality built directly into the materials. Customizable smart-materials point toward exciting applications for adaptive products, new shipping possibilities, and high-performance material systems.

In collaboration with: Shelly Linor, Daniel Dikovsky, and Shai Hirsch, Stratasys Ltd.; and Carlos Olguin, Autodesk, Inc.

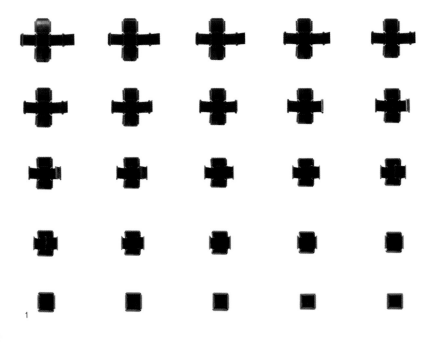

1

1: Step-by-step process of a 4-D printed surface transforming over time into a closed surface cube

2: 4-D printed strand transforming over time into a wireframe 3-D cube

3: 4-D printed strand transforming over time into the letters *MIT*

YOUNG PROJECTS
Bryan Young

152 **Playa Grande Main House**
158 **Playa Grande Bungalows**
160 **Gerken Loft**
168 **Photographer's Townhouse and Studio**
172 **Carraig Ridge Fireplace**
174 **Hive Lantern**

We interpreted "Range" as a diversity of language. Our aesthetic and compositional vocabulary is continuously evolving, varying from project to project and inclusive of multiple readings. Singularity is unnecessary—it bounds the potential for innovation and limits the range of work a young office might produce. We strive to operate free from any predetermined biases to conceptual values or stylistic trends that might begin to constrain an organic design process.

We are by circumstance a service-based office; by responding to parameters of site, context, budget, and constructability, our commissions are unified by their intention from day one to be constructed buildings. Although our designs are formally divergent, they remain connected by the very essence of their response to physical constraints. It is the deliberate consideration of material properties, deployment, and assembly techniques that yields a consistent methodology rather than a unifying aesthetic agenda. We utilize digital means, but are equally interested in reconsidering traditional methods of construction and inventing analog techniques, uncovering project loopholes, and celebrating glitches.

All of the projects presented here are complete, under construction, or breaking ground in the near future. We innovate through achievable means to create critical works derived from heightened attention to resources, awareness of site and vernacular, and reconsidered material assemblies.

Playa Grande Main House

Playa Grande, Dominican Republic, 2013

Located on an undeveloped site in the Dominican Republic, the Retreat at Playa Grande is designed to take advantage of the pristine beachscape at the front of the property, balancing expansive views of the Atlantic Ocean with the experience of the lush, dense jungle that dominates the majority of the site. Following natural shifts in topography, a visitor moves under the Main House and emerges up into the airy central courtyard where framed views of the ocean and horizon are finally revealed, eliciting a sense of arrival.

In the most diagrammatic sense, the Main House is a transformation of a courtyard parti. Directed by solar orientation, natural ventilation, and the desire to preserve primary existing trees and vegetation, the evolved form is a drifting ring that shifts in plan and section just below the jungle's canopy. The roof is a ruled surface requiring over two hundred scissor trusses; each is dimensionally unique but simple in joinery and construction. The result is a highly complex and fluid structural condition that shifts along the corridor, curves through primary double-height spaces, and rotates to navigate the geometry at each corner. The design facilitates a panoramic experience of the site, from its diverse jungle landscape to its vast ocean views.

1

1: View of entry

2: Roof plan

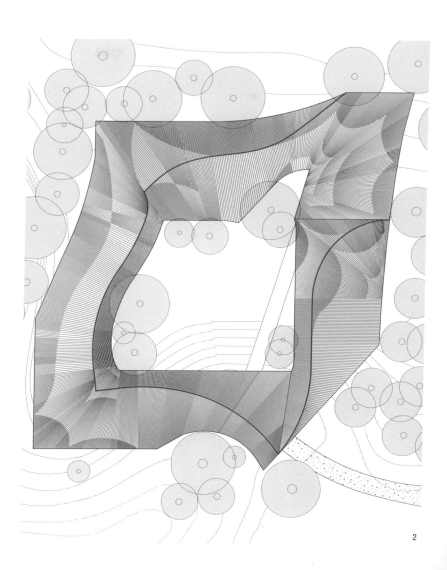

2

3: Ground floor plan
4: Unfolded elevation showing peeling of facade and roof

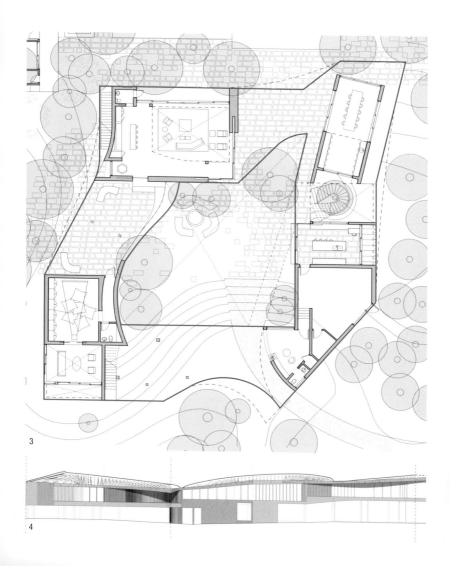

3

4

5: Second floor plan

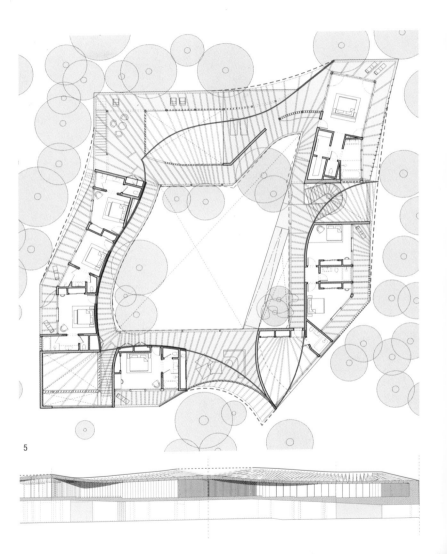

5

6: Axonometric of roof battens
7: Axonometric of scissor trusses
8: Batten generation diagrams

6

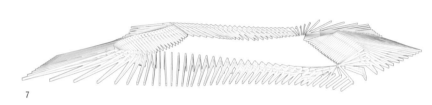

7

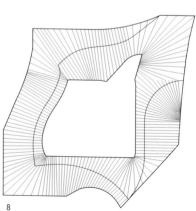

8

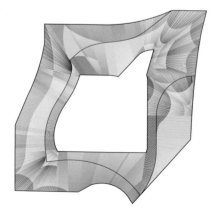

9: View of funroom
10: Exhibition model showing trusses and roof
11: View inside funroom

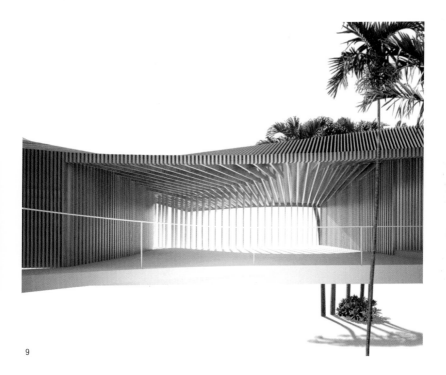

9

10

11

Playa Grande Bungalows

Playa Grande, Dominican Republic, 2013

Farther inland on the site, three freestanding bungalows slip through the existing growth of trees in a manner similar to the lifted meandering of the Main House. Their pleated walls create a highly textural surface within the jungle landscape. Each triangular fold balances the desires for privacy and view, and shades the glass behind from the strong midday sun to reduce heat gain. As each wall gently curves through the jungle, a fluttering rhythm of light and shadow diffuses sunlight into the interior spaces. The height of each pleat remains consistent at 3.75 meters; therefore, the mass of the bungalow becomes a direct offset of the topography below, monitoring existing and reconstructed ground conditions. The design is contemporary, yet its simple method of construction alludes to the vernacular craftsmanship of the Dominican Republic.

1: Wood pleat construction sequence
2: Panoramic view of bungalows in site
3: Full-scale mock-up of wood pleats

4: Detail view of bungalows
5: Site plan

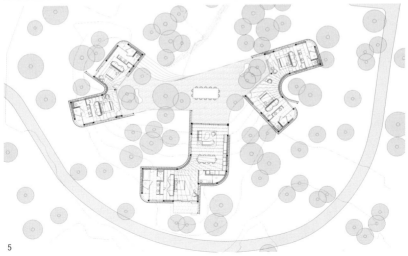

Gerken Loft
New York, New York, 2013

The Gerken Loft is 6,000 interior square feet occupying the thirteenth and fourteenth floors and 1,500 square feet of roof garden in a historic Tribeca building. The proposal explores shifting relationships of solid and void through the interplay of three nested prisms. At the entrance to the loft a massive courtyard cuts open to the sky and city. This initial void is subsequently revealed to be bounded by a larger cut through the fourteenth floor, allowing the courtyard to be read as a floating glass mass bridging the east and west sides of the plan and opening the section between floors. The larger cut also exposes the existing building core as a monolithic mass that grounds the choreography of adjacent, interconnected voids and solids. This core is clad in custom pulled-plaster panels, a technique developed through the controlled collision of a centuries-old fabrication technique with contemporary digital design language. The project is formally restrained but spatially provocative through the improbability of the empty courtyard positioned as a positive mass of air and landscape within the loft.

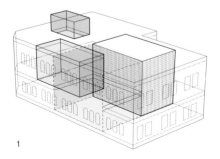

1

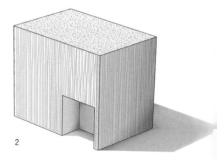

2

1: Massing composition of solids and voids
2: Monolithic plaster core volume

3: View of stair and courtyard from salon
4: View of bridge and courtyard from kitchen

5: View of bridge and courtyard from family room
6: View of tree shadow projection

7: Building section
8: Unfolded elevations of plaster tiles on core

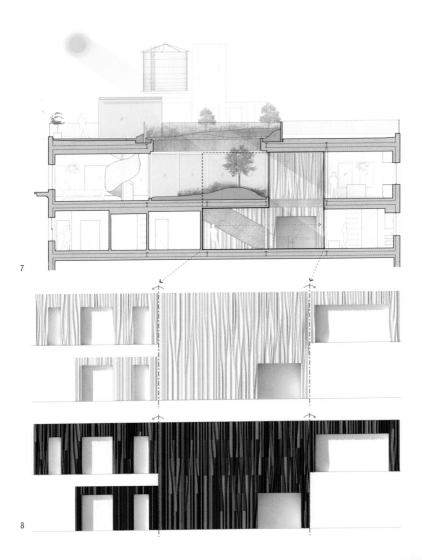

7

8

9–10: Modified plaster pulling process (our invention)
11–12: Swept plaster profiles
13: First pull

14: Ten minutes later...
15: Plaster prototype tile

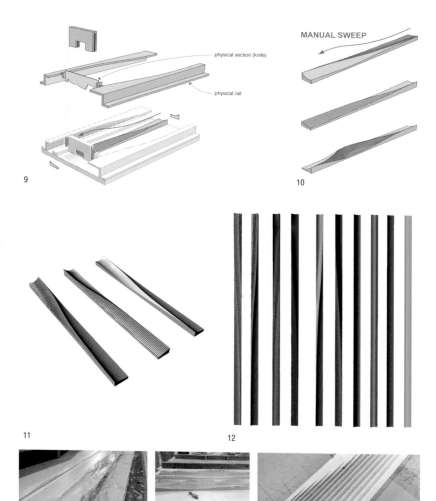

16: Detail of plaster tiles looking up
17: Detail of plaster tiles at stair handrail

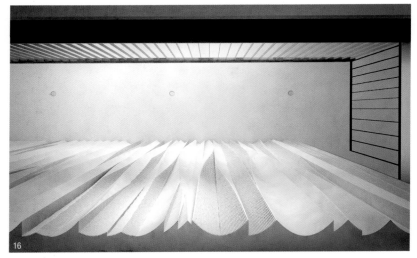

18–19: Break lines and surface geometries of spiral
20: Color projections on milled MDF fins

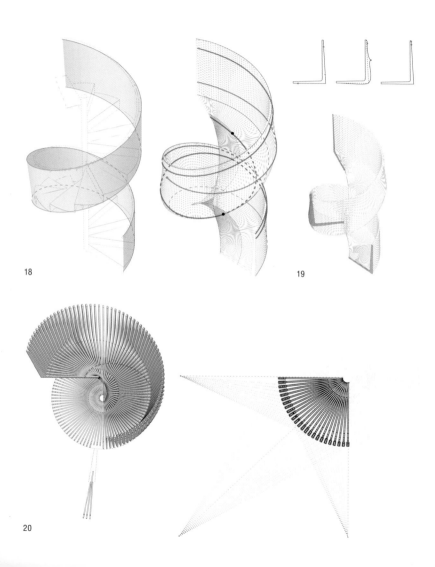

18

19

20

21: Spiral stair

Photographer's Townhouse and Studio

Brooklyn, New York, 2013

The Photographer's Townhouse and Studio involves a gut renovation and addition to an existing townhouse on a corner lot in Williamsburg, Brooklyn. To satisfy the client's aspirations of maintaining the existing commercial occupancy on the ground floor while maximizing residential space on the upper levels, the second floor was extended to create one continuous living zone sandwiched between sleeping above and working below. The addition hovers on pilotis above the backyard, bridging two traditional brick buildings while minimizing expensive excavation and foundation work. A corrugated zinc facade screens and unifies the two stacked volumes of the addition and contrasts the massive brickwork of the townhouse. The upper volume shifts off the existing structure to allow interior penetration of sunlight and create a sectional layering of roof gardens: a private courtyard on the third floor and a public one above. This composition of landscapes is visible through a glass clerestory in the adjacent double-height living room on the second floor of the existing townhouse.

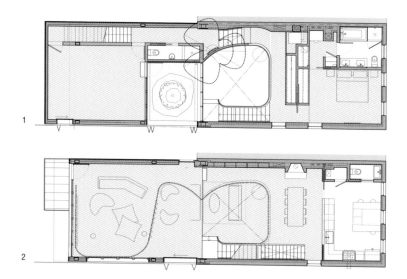

1

2

1: Third floor plan
2: Second floor plan

3: View from sidewalk
4: View across interior fault line

5: Building elevation
6: Building section

5

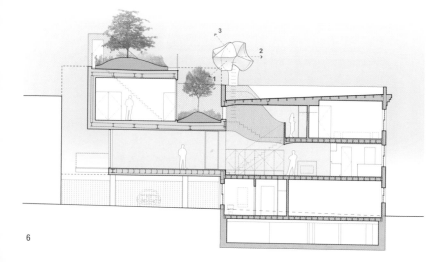

6

7: Orb (camera obscura) orientation and form

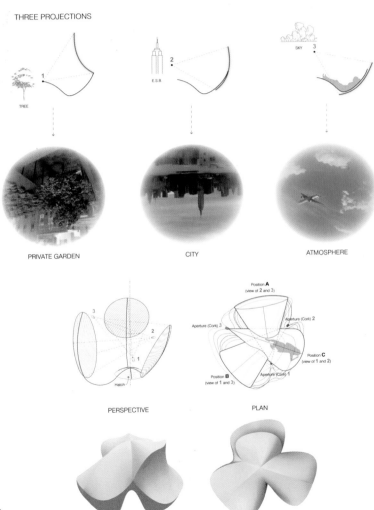

THREE PROJECTIONS

1 TREE

2 E.S.B.

SKY 3

PRIVATE GARDEN

CITY

ATMOSPHERE

PERSPECTIVE

PLAN

7

Carraig Ridge Fireplace
Carraig Ridge, Alberta, 2013

The Carraig Ridge Fireplace amplifies the conventional fire pit to create an inhabitable fireplace that functions as the hearth to the lake and surrounding hills. It is simultaneously a monumental landmark and destination, a beacon hovering above the lake, and very much a part of the site.

    With a limited design schedule of just four weeks, it was important to develop a straightforward method of construction using a readily available source of materials. As such, the Fireplace is constructed of local heavy timbers cut into lengths of three to five feet and stacked in six unique positions according to simple rules of rotation. This subtle twist is a playful interpretation of the traditional method of stacking logs, and produces a contemporary result that references the traditional log cabin but adds exaggerated intricacy and texture. This method creates a porous, thick surface that envelops the warmth of the fire but allows light to slip through to the outside, and provides users with moments of oblique views back to the landscape. The outside prismatic form is softened by the texture of the raw wood in contrast to the polished metal ends, scattering fragmented reflections of the surrounding water, earth, and sky into an ethereal veil. The Fireplace will be followed by a tree house and picnic house as part of a larger series of landscape follies.

1

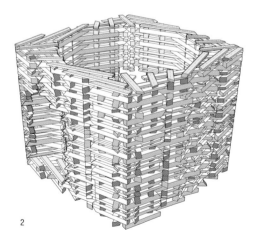

2

1–2: Construction, stacking, and massing diagrams

3: Fireplace in the landscape
4: Fireplace at night

Hive Lantern

New York, New York, 2010

While the Hive Lantern might seem to be a distant cousin of a beehive, it is actually more alien in its form and structure, relating to the biology of flowers (ovule, stigma, and petal) and imagery appropriated from science fiction. It consists of three spiraling lobes whose symmetry is obscured by an organic cellular structure that morphs across its surface. Varying cell sizes, shapes, and depths cast the light from three interior bulbs in a complex pattern.

The parametric definition is simple, packing six basic cell units around the spiraling lobe form. The pentagonal cells share centers, creating a fluctuating hierarchy on the surface in which center stigmas share circumscribing petals. The thickening and thinning of the Hive membrane is critical in order to control moments of increased light transmission while decreasing direct views to the bulbs. Each of the three lobes relates to one of the internal bulbs, selected to appear as unhatched seeds protected within.

Each Hive Lantern is 3-D printed from a digital model and plated in nickel. The Hive's outer faces are polished, suggesting the reading of a wind-weathered fossil. Since installing the Hives on a rooftop garden terrace, adjacent birch trees and landscape have begun to mask the stainless steel support rod. Eventually the Hives will be supported by the mature trees.

The Hive Lantern is the result of collaboration with Michael Young of the design firm Young & Ayata.

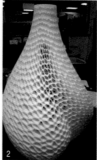

1: Cardboard study model
2: 3-D printed polymer prototype

3: Lanterns installed on rooftop
4: Lantern from below
5: Lanterns at night

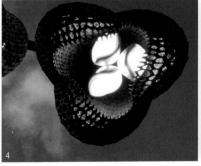